Clicking for Cash from Home

I0473626

By Laura L. Smith

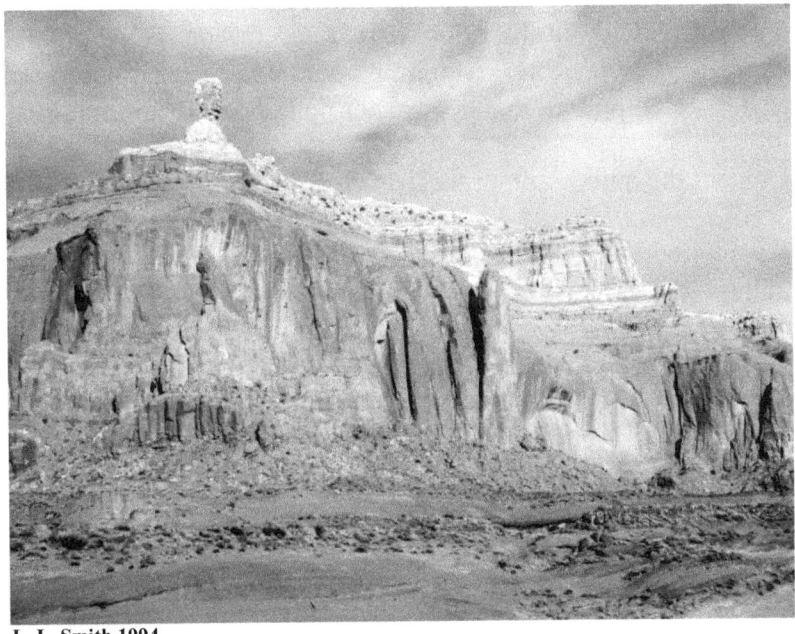

L. L. Smith 1994

1

Clicking for Cash from Home

Contact the author at laural.s2012@gmail.com

All photographs in book, unless referenced, are taken by the author

Other books by the author:

Adult Coloring Book Featuring Cats, Romance, Angel's & Flowers

Our Spiritual Awakening

Pink Kitty's Friendly Tales

The Cat Chat Forum

Clicking for Cash from Home

Table of Contents

Introduction

Thank-you for purchasing this affordable reader friendly guide in which I share my 20 years of photography business experience. My goal is to help you learn how to earn money working as a home-based professional photographer.

There are plenty of books on the market that will teach you how to take beautiful and stunning photos, but do not cover the business aspect of making money as a photographer.

Then there are books and magazines that cover how to make money in your photography business, but the content is focused more for the established professional photographer.

Plus, there are the countless photography websites flooding the Internet with varied and complicated photo taking and editing techniques.

Along with the expensive programs, that promise you will make thousands a month from selling photos you take on your kitchen table, without buying expensive equipment.

It can be downright overwhelming, confusing, and intimidating if you are starting out in photography. That is why I wrote this guide. It is geared to teach you how to take photos and run a business to earn you money.

Now, if you are planning upon starting out doing photography part-time, I strongly recommend you have your Friday nights and weekends free. As this is when the majority of weddings, family reunions, in home family portraits, company, anniversary, and birthday parties are held.

It is also important to understand that my guide is not one of these overnight routes to riches programs.

As with any business you want to be successful in, it requires a desire to invest the time, energy, money and work to learn how to be a good photographer and earn money.

You also need to be a people person who enjoys interacting with people and their families, plus the occasional crowd.

And, you should have good communication and sales skills as you will be selling your services.

Plus you should be a person who loves photography and already have a natural talent or flair for taking photos, because if you love what you do it shows in your work.

So in order to have the tools to make money, in this guide I cover topics on:

- The photography equipment and easy-to-use inexpensive editing software you need and where to buy it

- How to photograph weddings, portraits, school groups, social and business parties, pets, and product.

- Developing a website that will have people calling to hire you

- How to get into stock photography

- How to price your services and get free advertising through the websites brides visit

- How to be an effective sales person by listening and knowing when to use the art of small talk

- A chapter on free to use promotional materials, photo and pricing sheets and agreement form templates

- How to develop B & W film and print fine art photos

All websites mentioned in this guide can be found in the appendix of this guide.

Chapter 1 THE BASICS

1.1 No Degree Needed

You don't need a four year college photography degree to be a successful home-based photographer. However, just like singing, acting, or playing an instrument—photography is an art form that requires a certain level of natural born talent or flair to be successful.

And if you are a person who receives positive feedback from people you show your photos to, sounds like you may already have that talent.

So it would make sense that you are taking the next step to learn how to make money using that talent.

The same holds true for salesmanship which requires that you have both listening and good conversation skills, have a likeable and trusting personality, and the ability to make your client feel as though she/he is the only one you have.

Myself, back in the day before digital, I completed three college semesters in black and white film photography plus one commercial photography course. I enjoyed the hands on experience developing film and making prints. Plus I got plenty of real time critique on my work from my instructors who worked as professional photographers.

In the commercial photography class I learned more advanced photo techniques and a few marketing and sales tips.

However, I am going to share a secret with you about what the photography schools will never admit to…

You don't have to take several photography classes, or as a matter of fact, go out and spend thousands of dollars to obtain a four year degree to be a professional photographer.

Because, during my entire twenty years of being in business, I had approximately two inquiries about my educational background. One inquiry was from a couple who were doctors, and when they found out I did not have a photography degree, they did not hire me.

The other inquiry came from a man who was interviewing me to photograph his wedding. He stated that he had training from the Brooks Institute of Photography and grilled me on what my education credentials were. When he looked at my portfolio books, he leaned over the open album and took his finger and ran it down the page as if he was reading brail.

Even though his actions puzzled me, I answered his questions. In the end he did not hire me, which saved me from telling him that someone else hired me for his date.

However, if your goal is to be a photographer for a magazine such as Sports Illustrated, or a newspaper like the New York Times, or to work for a major advertising company as their photographer, then you will need a degree.

1.2 Client Diversity

As a freelance home-based wedding and event photographer, you will be contacted by people of all races, religions, and belief systems. This means having to evaluate your own assumptions and prejudges to decide if you are able to put them aside so you can do a good job. If you are not able to, that is fine, it just means that you will be limited in the type of jobs you accept. The following are the different types of lifestyles and religions that you may encounter:

- **ALTERNATE LIFESTYLES & BELIEFS**—Regardless of our opinions on marriage, gay and lesbian weddings are here to stay. I have photographed gay weddings where the families of the couple were in attendance and supportive. And as far as interracial couples, in this day and time, that should not even be an issue.

  And at one reception, a groomsman had a tee shirt on under his white tux shirt that read *Desert association of Skin*

Heads. I don't like the Neo Nazi philosophy, but I kept quiet as it was not the time or place to say anything.

- **MUSLIM RELIGION:** The family will get together for the reading from the Koran and cake cutting. Afterwards the men and women go to separate rooms for the reception. The veiled women will expose their face and allow photos with the bride and other women. These women would then ask me if there would be men looking at the photos at the film processors. This is because no man outside the family can look at the woman's face. I had to assure them that only women processed the photos. I was allowed to go into the men's area because I was a westerner and not a Muslim.

- **MORMONS**—For a temple wedding, the bridal couple, their bridal party, and family must be bona fide card carrying members of the Mormon church to be part of the ceremony. Photography is not allowed during a temple ceremony. After a temple wedding, bridal party and family photos are taken outside on the grounds in front of the temple. This is because Mormon families are supposed to have a photo of the nearest temple hanging in their home. If the bridal couple wants to have non-Mormon guests at their wedding ceremony, it is held at a ward. Again there is no photography during the ceremony.

- **ETHNIC WEDDINGS**—A Mexican wedding ceremony can be as long as 1.5 hours. The reception—which can last up to seven or more hours, usually starts with serving food and mariachis playing music. Then there is a DJ until the live band starts playing. Eastern European Orthodox weddings can last up to two and a half hours and the reception up to seven or more hours.

1.3 Business Resources

When you are starting in any business—you need guidance and resources to help you get going. But you don't have to pay a personal consultant thousands of dollars when the government has business organizations that offer free or low cost business advice.

The **Small Business Administration** (SBA) website learning center offers a variety of courses covering topics in taxes, marketing, sales, and advertising. It can be found under the **tools/sba-learning-center/search/training/starting-business link on their website**.

This site also has a link that lists your local SBA District Office offering counseling, mentoring, and training from **SCORE** (Service Core of Retired Executives) and the Small Biz Development Center or Women's Biz Center in your area.

Plus are you aware that the IRS has free information on setting up your taxes for small business? It can be found under the **Small-Businesses-&-Self-Employed/Starting-a-Business link**.

To build up a portfolio, most people will photograph their family or friend's weddings and other events free or for a nominal fee to cover expenses. When they have a diverse portfolio and are confident in their skills, then the person begins to charge more and they may deposit the money into their personal checking account. However, once you gain a reputation and the jobs keep coming in and the money begins to exponentially add up, it has passed over from the hobby status to a business.

Which means, continuing to deposit monies earned from photo jobs into your personal account might raise red flags plus you can't write off your business expenses such as:
- *Photography equipment, software*
- *Office equipment and supplies such as ink and paper*
- *Advertising, promotional materials, and bridal shows*
- *Gas, car lease payments, insurance, mileage, and travel*
- *Business and health insurance*
- *Business organization fees, meals and entertainment*
- *Phone and Internet costs*

When reaching the hobby to business tipping point, it's time to consider whether to be a sole proprietor, have a partnership, or a limited liability corporation (LLC). My business was an LLC based upon the following information I researched.

So what is a sole proprietorship? These are one owner businesses and may have employees. The owner is responsible for all business transactions, can go out of business, or sell it or pass it on down to other family members.

Taxes are paid as part of the owner's individual income tax filing, and depending upon the location you live in, the business may need to be licensed.

What I did not like about the sole proprietorship was that I, the owner, would be liable for all business debts. So, if my business was unable to cover my debts, creditors would be able to come after my personal assets. I also would have faced the possibility of paying higher taxes as my profits increased.

Plus, as a sole proprietor, I couldn't deduct my health insurance expenses when filing my tax return.

As far as the partnership route, it is too much like being married to someone. You and your partner are equal owners in the assets and money. This means that if your partner decides to spend all the money and puts the business into debt, you are just as responsible. And that is why…

I chose an LLC and had a friend help me set it up using an on line do-it-yourself legal service to incorporate. I don't recall the name of the company, but the one that I hear advertised all the time is **Legal Zoom.** Like the site my friend used, legal zoom guides you through the set up process for a fee.

The advantages of the LLC I liked were that if anyone ever filed a personal judgment against me, they could not come after my business assets, and vice versa. Additionally, my LLC itself was not responsible for taxes on the profits, but instead I reported my profit and loss on my personal tax returns. And I didn't have to file a corporate tax return.

Also LLC's do not require you to be a United States citizen. Plus, it might be easier to get additional funding as it provides better credibility to prospective partners, clients, and lenders in comparison to the sole proprietorship.

An LLC requires filing your taxes by March 15 of each year. I didn't know that and missed the deadline one year and had to pay a $100.00 fine to the IRS.

For my bookkeeping, I used **Quickbooks**. On the site they offer a plan where you pay by the month and choosing the bookkeeping options you need. Or you can buy the software program which costs a few hundred dollars.

I also used the H & R Block business tax software which can transfer your QuickBooks information into the program.

However, if you are not tax savvy and do not like preparing returns, have it prepared by a tax accountant professional.

1.4 The Client's personal information

In your photography business you will be collecting client's sensitive information such as names, addresses, phone numbers, and credit card information.

Are you aware that the Federal Trade Commission (FTC) has stringent rules and regulations that businesses must follow on safeguarding client's personal and financial information? Because if your client's sensitive information is stolen and used by the wrong people, the client could sue to hold you financially responsible. Plus you might have to provide a credit monitoring service which can be quite costly. You may also be fined.

But you can avoid this business disaster by implementing safeguards to protect your client's information. First, you should already have your own dedicated business computer with a secure password and not allow unauthorized people who are not employees to have access to your computer files.

Case in point, a business acquaintance of mine who has an IT business received a call from a client to come fix her business computer. He went to her office and found viruses and malware from free downloaded games off the Internet. When he inquired who else was using the computer, the lady answered that when her grandkids visited, she let them play games on the computer.

My acquaintance explained to the woman that she was legally bound to safeguard her client's sensitive information and should not allow her grandkids to play on or download games onto her business computer. The lady stated that her grandkids were not interested in accessing her client's files.

That lackadaisical attitude is definitely not the way to run a business.

Maybe you are considering or are already using off line storage sites such as The I-Cloud, Just Cloud, Carbonite, Mozy, Dropbox, SOS On line backup, etc. You pay to upload your computer data files which are encrypted at least three times before being transmitted to the company's servers— where ever in the world they may be.

Myself, I would not use an offline storage data service. My thinking is, that anytime I send or upload sensitive data over a network, it is vulnerable to being hacked during transmission, even if it is encrypted.

It is also recommended not to store a client's sensitive information on a flash drive and carry it all over the place with you. Or worse yet, leave the flash drive where it is vulnerable to being stolen or lost.

As far as credit card slips, once the money from a transaction is deposited in your bank account, shred the credit card slip. Plus do not type in credit card numbers on the invoices that are being mailed to the client. And when you no longer need the invoices they should be deleted off your computer and not backed up onto an external hard drive or DVDs. Instead make hard paper copies for your records.

The FTC has a PDF on protecting client's sensitive information at **business.ftc.gov/documents/bus69-protecting-personal-information-guide-business**

Smart Tip: To protect your sensitive information, instead of using your home address on business cards, and other promotional marketing materials…Rent a mail box at a mail box store that has a street address, not a P.O. box number.

Saving Your Photo Jobs

To keep track of photo jobs on your computer, set up a folder for the current year. Then create subfolders categorized by weddings, portraits, and business jobs for that year.

Next create subfolders of individual jobs by client name and date. Then create for each job a raw and edited folder. Have a separate folder for DVD slide shows.

Keep the raw photo folder until all reorders from a job are completed before deleting.

Use DVD's instead of CD's to store the edited jobs. DVD's can hold up to 1200 images—about four jobs.

1.5 Leaving ego out of the picture

When photographing weddings, you will be directing people by doing the following:

Calling people up to the front of the church for the formal photos and telling them where to stand

Assembling families at the reception for photos

Telling the bridal couple what poses to do and where to stand for photos, how to do the toast, cut the cake, and throw the bouquet and garter

But sometimes photographers allow their egos to interfere, and they become insistent that clients must do what the photographer wants, as the photographer knows what is best. However, all this does is upset people, which results in no future business or referrals.

The best to avoid becoming an ego driven and demanding photography is to remember that:

"I am a professional photographer being paid to produce good quality product. I am also required to be polite and courteous. If I do have an idea I will pass the idea by the bridal couple for their approval. Either they will love it or if they will say no—I will smile and say okay and leave it at that. Because I am being paid to do what the client wants, not what I think is right."

<u>Other People's Ego</u>

As a photographer you probably will encounter professional jealousy from other photographers. These are the photographers who will have to prove just how much better a photographer they are then you.

However, do not let the insecurities of a few photographers get to you. Remind yourself that when someone has to prove how bad you are to boast their poor self esteem, they have a problem not you. Your best bet is to not play into the insecurities of others by arguing back. Instead take what they say with a grain of salt and remove yourself from the situation.

Here are three examples of my encounters with insecure photographers:

<u>Years ago I joined</u> an on-line photography chat room where I was the only female. When a visitor asked a question, the men answered with complicated photography techniques, data, and formulas whereas I wrote short and simple answers.

When the visitors thanked me for my answer, this got the men riled up and they embarked on a barrage of evidenced based rebuttals to prove me wrong. One Pulitzer Prize photographer called me a bumbling amateur that needed to get out of the chat room and I gladly took his advice.

My ex in-laws traveled all over the world. The father-in-law took hundreds of slides and boasted how his photos were as good as what he saw in National Geographic. One year right before Christmas I did my first paid photo job using my medium format camera. This bothered my father-in law and he had to prove how much more professional he was then me.

On Christmas day my then husband, our kids, and I went over to his parent's house for dinner. During the meal the father-in-law began talking about how he got all his pictures without using fancy equipment, and that he was going to set up the slide projector after dinner to show everyone his slides.

I kept quiet because had I said anything, he would have laughed and made a derogatory comment.

After dinner my then husband, his grandma and aunt, my kids and I retreated to the family room to watch television. My mother-in-law, two sisters-in-law, step brother-in-law, and his wife watched the show.

I could hear my ex-father-in- law repeating loudly from the living room about how his photos were as good as the ones he had seen in National Geographic. After 45 minutes he and the rest of the group entered the family room. The father-in-law looked at me and said, "You know Laura, you missed a great opportunity to see what real professional photos look like."

I then look at the father-in-law and said with a smile, "You know, you ought to submit your professional slides to National Geographic, they might even publish them." A hush came over the room as everyone looked at me.

The ex-father-in law then gave me a glare and tersely said as he sat down, "I don't need to submit my photos or buy a fancy camera to prove how good I am at photography."

After that day, my ex father-in-law never tried again to prove how much more professional he was then me.

One time I attended an amateur photography group meeting thinking it would be a good way to network. Two of my single friends accompanied me in hopes of meeting single men.

At the registration table two people gave us name tags to wear and provided us with the clubs information. I had brought along my 4" x 6" portable professional photo album that held a hundred photos.

As I mingled through the group, two older women stopped me and asked to see my photos. After looking at about ten photos they closed the album, handed it back to me, said a flat thank you, then walked away over to a large group of people and began talking to them.

My friends and I made our way over to several long tables that featured the member's mounted photos. As I was looking at the photos, the two women who had looked at my album, walked over to a table behind us. They began talking loudly about how professional looking and beautiful each other's photos were.

It then dawned on me that the women were jealous of my photography and I smiled. My one friend leaned over and commented under her breath, "They have got to be kidding, these photos look average and boring, I'm not impressed."

A few minutes later the three of us sat down to an hour long judged slide show presentation of the same photos. I dozed off midway through the show.

Right after the slide show we three left the building. Outside before parting to our separate cars, we voice our disappointment and decided that the photo club was not worth a return visit.

Chapter 2 PHOTO EQUIPMENT

2.1 The Equipment

Your first jobs will likely be weddings and on location portraits that require the use of an external flash set-up.

Below is a chart listing the equipment you need for your business. Prices are not listed as they change over time.

The highlighted red items are what you should buy first. The rest of the items can be purchased later as you bring in more money.

Equipment
2 digital Canon 35 mm with 18 – 55 mm lens and video feature
PC with 500 GB
Negative scanner and printer
Sigma DG 28 – 300 mm lens
Sunpack or Vivitar camera flashes—2
Sync cords & hot shoes adapters—2
Lumedyne external battery packs—2
Stroboframe's—2
Gary Fong Whale Tail diffuser
Speedotron Black line Studio lights
Canvas and muslin backdrops,
Photoshop CS suite
Paint shop pro
Pinnacle Studios DVD movie
Virtual painter

Here is a list of websites to purchase the equipment in the list above. The websites are also listed in the Appendix.

- **Adobe** Website for Photoshop CS

- **Adorama**—they sell lenses, Speedotron lighting, flash equipment, Lumedyne batteries, and Stroboframe's.

- **Backdrop Outlet**—Sells canvas and muslin backdrops. On page 33 there are instructions on how to make a muslin backdrop.

- **Corel**--Sells the Paint Shop Pro editing software

- **En.softonic Virtual-painter-5**—Virtual Painter software

- **Gary Fong Store**—This company sells the Gary Fong Whale Tail and Fong Soft drop and drag flush album software

- **Pinnaclesys.com**—Website for Pinnacle Studios Movie and DVD slide show software

- **Sams Club**—they sell cameras, printers, scanners, PCs and offer low cost photo printing.

- **Speedotron** Sells studio lighting

You should have a computer that has at least 500 GB. The average 35 mm camera JPEG image is about 1 to 1.3 MB. The average amount of wedding photos taken at a job is around 415 images. And that will double when you make the edited file folder in addition to the raw image file folder. So if you are doing three weddings a weekend plus other photo jobs during the week, it adds up.

Plus the average DVD slide show of a wedding can be 25 minutes and take up as much as 515 MB. Then you have your photo editing and movie making software, and other photography related items.

You will also notice that on many of these websites there are specialized books and tutorials on how to take wedding and commercial photography, nudes, portraits, scenery, etc. However, once you learn the basics of positioning your camera, focusing, metering, framing, cropping in the lens, lighting, and posing your subject, you will be able to photograph all types of situations.

Additionally, you need to understand that the point and shoot (P & S) cameras are unsuitable for professional use. They do not have the manual settings, raw image ability, inter-changeable lenses and on camera hot shoes.

Not only that, but if you show up at a paying job with even a high end P & S camera, the people who hired you will give you a look of dismay and say, *"Seriously, is that the camera you're using? Had I known that, I could have saved a lot of money by shooting the pictures myself!"*

Even though the Canon Rebel is the camera listed, you should choose the brand you will be comfortable shooting with. Canon also sells a high end 35 mm with more megapixels and features. These cameras are popular with commercial photographers and photojournalists.

The new model Rebel cameras also have video capability that allows photographers to record events. It used to be that before affordable video cameras came onto the market, people would spend up to $600.00 to hire a professional videographer to record events. Today most photography companies offer both video and still photography as a package together.

Plus, there is affordable movie making software such as the **Pinnacle Studio** Series that is easy to use.

However, there will always be a need for the talented wedding photographer to capture beautiful and unique wedding, event, and portrait photos.

2.2 Lenses and Aperture

There is a variety of lenses with different price ranges depending upon the manufacturer, fast maximum aperture lens opening i.e. f/2.8, focal length, vibration reduction, and quality of glass and coatings used for the lens.

When you buy larger lenses with maximum apertures such as f/1.4, 2.8, spherical aberration can occur. This is an optical problem where all incoming light rays end up focusing at different points after passing through the lens.

Even though this guide is about making money and not how lenses are built, aperture needs to be understood for metering photos and using print enlargers. The following information from the Nikon website explains lens aperture.

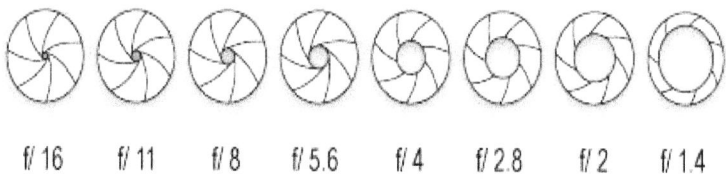

f/ 16   f/ 11   f/ 8   f/ 5.6   f/ 4   f/ 2.8   f/ 2   f/ 1.4

Nikon Aperture Image

"*Aperture refers to the opening of a lens's diaphragm through which light passes. It is calibrated in f/stops and is written as numbers i.e. 1.4, 2, 2.8, 4, 5.6, 8, 11, and 16. Using a lower f/stop will create a larger lens opening, less depth of field, and a blurrier background. The higher the f/stop will result in a smaller lens opening, a greater the depth of field resulting in a sharper background*"[1](Nikon 2014).

The light weight Canon EOS Rebel kit comes with an EFS 18 to 55 mm lens. The light weight Rebel helps keep the arms from getting tired while holding up the camera, Stroboframe, and flash set up.

The lens wide angle and close-up capabilities are suitable for photographing large wedding parties, sports teams, school groups, portraits, and close-up or macro photography.

The Rebel Kit sold at Sams Club, includes a zoom lens, but it lacks the wide angle shooting range needed for large groups. It is best suited for close-up and macro photography.

For outdoor and travel photography I use a heavier SIGMA 28-300 mm lens with a 1:35–6:3 aperture. I used the wide angle capability for scenery shots and the 300 mm focal length for zooming in on people and other scenes from a distance.

Even though the lens has wide angle capability, I find it impractical for photographing weddings and portraits. The additional weight tires the arms plus I have to hold the lens which causes slight movement of the camera adding a slight blur to the photo.

2.3 Flash Equipment

Most weddings, portraits, showers, birthdays, and company parties are photographed indoors. This requires an external flash system instead of using the on camera flash, or inserting a flash unit into the cameras hot shoe. The reason for not using these two flash methods is it causes direct flash.

Direct flash creates shiny spots, and harsh glare on people's faces, shadows behind and to the side of subjects, and washes out lighter items such as light colored clothing, wedding cake icing, and wrapping paper.

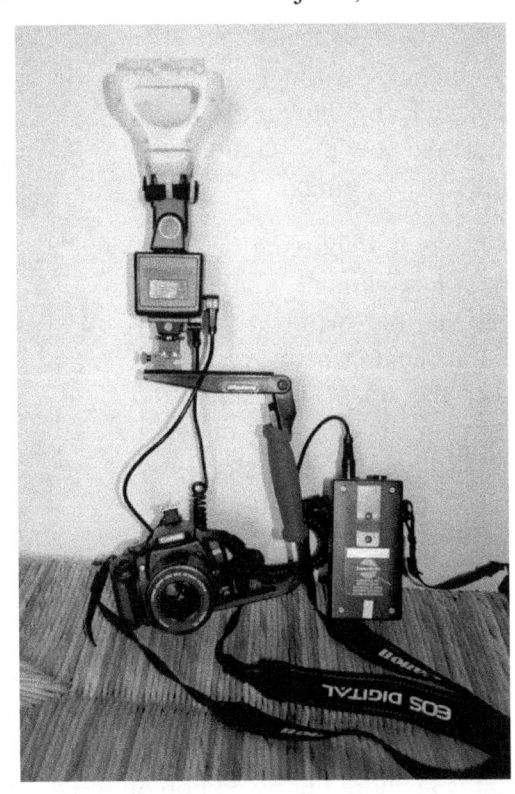

The first photo here shows an example of an external flash set up. The purpose of this flash set up is to eliminate the direct flash faux pas.

The white item on top of the flash set up is the **Gary Fong Whale Tail.** A Velcro strap attaches the whale tail onto the top portion of the flash.

The flash unit is a Sunpack with a movable and rotating upper section. This allows the photographer to point it towards the ceiling and create bounce flash instead of direct flash. The flash unit is attached onto the Stroboframe which is screwed into the bottom of the camera.

The second photo here is a close up of the Gary Fong Whale Tail diffuser and flash unit. This diffuser is an older style and there are newer updated products on the site.

The concept of the whale tail is to spread out and diffuse the light to eliminate the direct flash look. The result is your photos will look like you were using studio lighting.

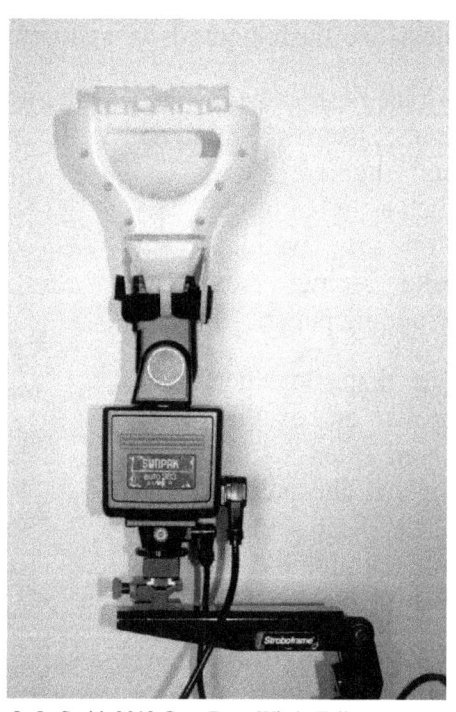

A matter of fact, it replaced my having to haul and use my studio lights at weddings.

What is not showing on the Gary Fong Whale Tail is the white flap that can either be moved over the open side slot seen in the photo, or onto the open top slot for more diffused lighting.

L. L. Smith 2013 Gary Fong Whale Tail

On the side of the flash unit there are two ports. The top port is for one end of the **Lumedyne battery** cord and the lower port is for the flash sync cord. The one end of the flash sync cord fits into a hot shoe adapter that slides into the hot shoe on top of the camera. The flash unit is pushed into a hot shoe adaptor that is anchored in by a knob on the flash bracket that is on top of the Stroboframe.

The Stroboframe is the C shape item that screws into the bottom of the camera. The top arm moves upward to keep the flash above the camera when you turn the camera vertical which…

Eliminates the typical amateur photographer's method of pushing the flash into the hot shoe on top of the camera, and bending the top part of the flash towards the subject that,

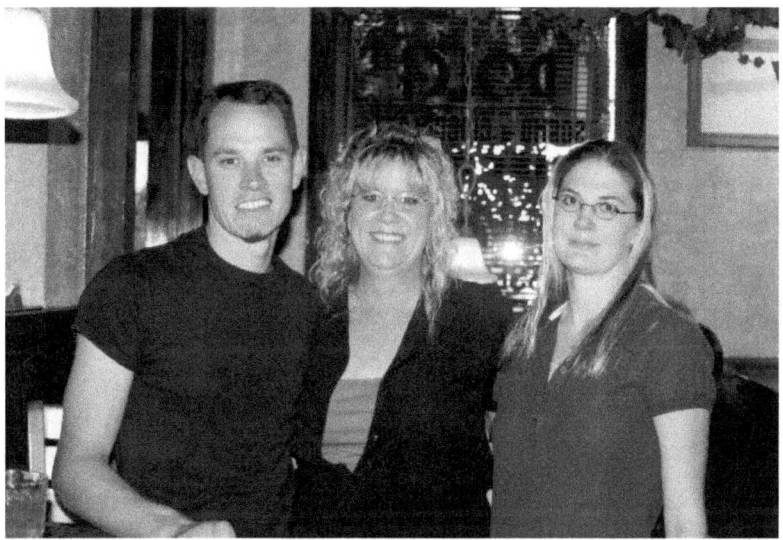

L. L. Smith (2006) Son, sister & daughter Liz

Results in the type of photo above. The direct flash photo of my son, sister, and daughter above casts a harsh light effect and shiny areas on their faces and they also look flattened. Plus, there is a shadow by my son's right ear and a flash dot on the window between my sister and daughter.

To avoid flash dots, don't pose people in front of reflective surfaces. However with that said, a person at an event may approach and direct you to a group of people they have already posed in front of a glass or reflective wall.

The best solution then is to move the group to another area to avoid the light from your flash above the heads in the mirror faux pas. Plus you will save time editing out the flash from the glass.

Also when using direct flash, if there is no plain light colored wall behind the people to reflect the light back, the area behind them will be dark and the photo will lack depth.

The photo of my son and his friend below is taken with bounce flash using the Gary Fong Whale Tail. Note how the light is diffused and fills in the area behind them giving depth to the image.

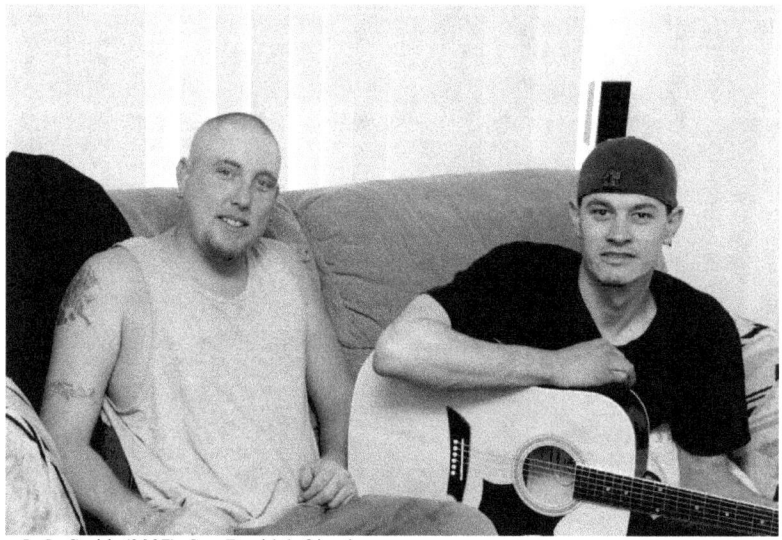

L. L. Smith (2007) Son David & friend

The photo on the next page is of the Lumedyne battery which costs about $300.00, but can be purchased for less on sites like EBay.

The Lumedyne battery pack comes with chargers and the flash cords depending upon the external camera flash brand you specify. The battery can pay for itself within the first year and a half, depending upon the amount of jobs you do.

Before I bought a Lumedyne battery I would buy the 48 AA count battery packages from Sams Club at a cost of $20.00. I shot about 52 weddings a year and went through about 12 AA batteries a wedding. So I did the math and discovered I was going to save money buying a Lumedyne battery.

- 12 batteries x 52 wedding = 624 batteries.
- 624 batteries divided by 48 packages = 13 packages a year.
- 13 packages x $20.00 = **$260.00!**

Now mind you, this estimation did not include the other photography jobs I did throughout the year.

L. L. Smith (2013)

So needless to say, the cost savings advantage of the Lumedyne was, I did not have to buy batteries to haul around and throw away.

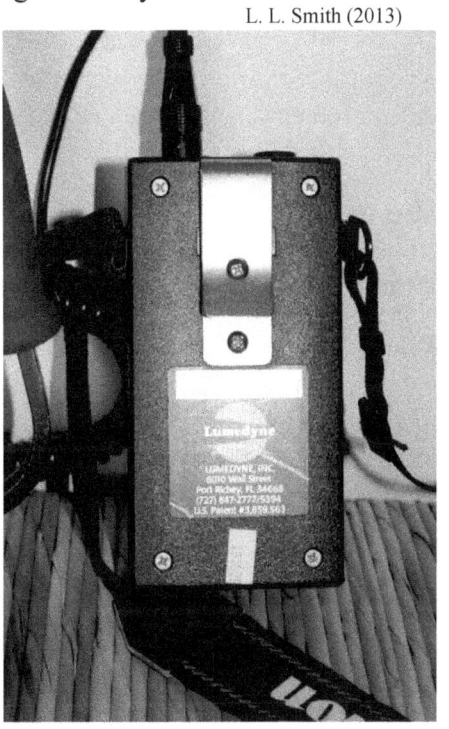

Another Lumedyne advantage is, it has a two second flash recharge cycle time. The AA batteries have a slower five second cycle time.

A five second recycle time is too long during fast moving events such as the wedding processional/recessional, cake cutting, and bouquet and garter tosses.

2.4 Be Prepared—Have extra and back it up

As a professional photographer, you will need additional back-up equipment in case of equipment failure. Even then you may still have prospective clients asking "Do you have back-up or extra equipment?"

Now this could be one of those moments when you have to avoid the knee-jerk egotistic reaction of "well, yeah, duh." But instead you smile and reply, "Why yes I do," and explained the following information to the client:

I bring three cameras with me

When photographing a wedding at a site that does not allow flash during the ceremony, mount the secondary camera on your tripod so it is ready to go. The camera used for taking flash photos can be kept over your shoulder during the ceremony.

When the ceremony is over, the tripod is then moved aside and the camera with the flash is pulled up to take the kissing and recessional photos.

Also, so that people will not trip over and knock down your tripod when exiting the church, take a moment and move it out of the way.

When photographing at a church with a loft, set up your tripod and camera so during the homily or sermon you can go upstairs to take photos. Then quietly bring your setup downstairs and set it aside.

And the reason for a third camera? Digital cameras can and do stop working.

I bring two batteries, flashes, the accessories, and CF cards

Years ago, I was the photographer for a renaissance wedding center and wore a long skirt as part of my outfit. During a reception I squatted down by my camera bag to get more film. When I stood up I stepped on the skirt hem and fell forward. The Lumedyne in my hand hit the tile floor and broke the interior electronics. I was glad I had two more with me.

When flashes, flash cables, and hot shoe adaptors are going bad they will start misfiring intermittently before they quit working. I had a CF card crash during a non-paying event and I lost the photos.

Backing up the photos

It's late and you have just gotten home tired out from a six hour photo job and just want to go to bed. But before you do, you should download your photos and make a back up CD because you can't afford to lose them, and besides...

Anything can happen between the end of the job and the next morning. Computers do and can crash at any time, the CF card could crap out, or worse yet your photos get deleted. One time my daughter deleted my photos of a trip to Mexico, but fortunately I had already sent the files over to Sams Club to make prints.

2.5 Studio Lighting and Accessories

I soon discovered that without studio lighting, I was not able to obtain jobs photographing company holiday parties, office groups, my in home business portraits, products, church, school groups, and other similar jobs. In other words, I was losing profits.

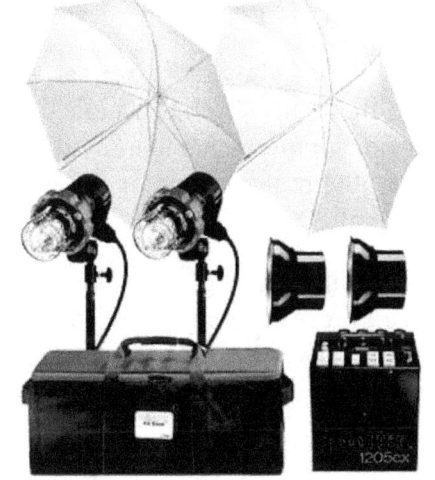

So in 1990 I purchased a Speedotron Black Line lighting system for $1600.00. When I sold the lights in 2010 for $850.00, the original light bulbs were still intact.

And the reason for that was, I attached and kept the 7" reflectors on the light heads when I was not using my dome light and during storage .

However, at the time of this writing, a Black Line system from **B & H photo**[2] now costs around $2800.00. This kit includes a 1205CX - 1200 W/S Power Pack, 2-202VF Color Corrected Flash Heads, Umbrellas, Sync Cord, Stands, 3-Section Air Case (B & H 2014).

When handling the modeling light bulbs that come with the kit, wear clean cloth gloves or use a soft clean cloth. This prevents skin oils from getting on the bulbs.

I also bought a 34" by 45" **Photoflex light dome**[3] that I began using in addition to the umbrellas for photo jobs, portraits, and product shots. It prevented the round light dots that would show up on reflective surfaces such as people's eye glasses.

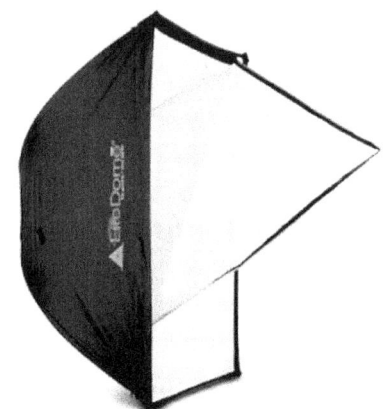

When I first bought my studio lights my 35 mm Canon film cameras did not have the electronic components that my digital cameras had. In order to prevent the high voltage of the studio lights from burning out the digital electronics—I used a low Voltage Sync Adapter.

Additionally you should always be safe and turn off the power source before pushing in or pulling out the lamp head cables from the power source. This can save your power source from being damaged.

Another lighting accessory that I purchased from Adorama was the **Smith Victor PG6S Mini Slave.**[4]

This item was placed on the ground behind the subject and added fill light that highlighted the canvas behind my subjects. The mini slave went off at the same time as the main and hair lights fired.

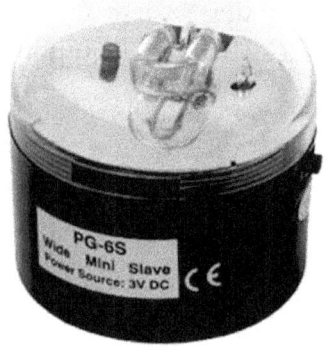

I made a home studio by setting up my studio lights and my 8 ft x 8 ft canvas backdrop in my living room. Clients would come by to have their portraits taken and afterwards I would download the photos onto my computer to burn a CD.

I didn't have to spend time editing the photos because what I saw in the camera view back was how it would look on the disc. After burning the images onto a CD, I collected my $150.00 for an hour's work and the client left with their CD.

2.6 The Light Box

In the 1990's I made my own product light box with PVC piping and joints. It measured 2 ft x 2 ft x 2 ft and I taped architect's tracing paper to all the sides except the front. I taped a piece of blue background paper onto the back side.

But you don't have to reinvent the wheel, as you can buy a complete light tent set up from Adorama for under $50.00.

The photo here shows their Table top Photo Studio in a bag with 16" x 16" Soft Light Box, Halogen Lamps, Blue/White Background Sweep, Camera Stand w/ carry case.

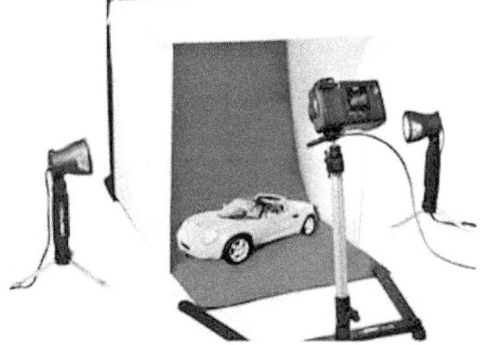

The Adorama website ad reads:
"Light weight and easy to set up table top design, the soft light box utilizes a specially woven, heat resistant, 100% nylon fiber mesh diffuser, which delivers uniform illumination while eliminating harsh shadows and reflective glare. Folds up for convenient storage and travel." [5]

Now as you can see from the photo, even though this portable table top set up has lights, they don't have the lighting capabilities like a studio lighting system.

31

Adorama also sells larger light tents such as 24" x 24" x 24" Interfit Photographic Studio Light Box for Larger Product Shots, for under $50.00.

A light box works great when photographing glass, jewelry, or a metal item. The material acts as a scrim to diffuse the light and avoids causing glare. To create a reflection of the items underneath, place a piece of dark shiny Plexiglas under the object. I would place my light dome about 2 to 2.5 ft feet directly over the top of my homemade light box—then metered the light hitting the object and took the photo.

2.7 Light Meters

Using studio lights requires the use of a light meter. Pricing can range from under $100.00 up to $500.00. Basically, you want a meter that is easy to use and gives you a reading when the lights fire.

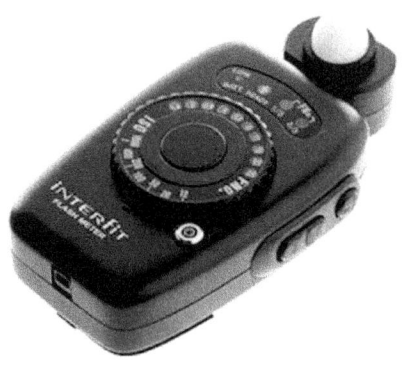

The image featured here is the Interfit Photographic FM-01, Digital Incident and Reflected Flash Meter priced under $50.00 at Adorama.[6]

And unlike the higher ASA camera settings used for indoor external flash photos, using an ASA setting of 100 on the flash meter works well for studio lighting.

2.8 Storage Bin & Hauling Cart

The metal studio light storage bins can be pricey. What I used to store my studio light was to purchase a heavy duty plastic truck bed tool box with a locking lid from a big box self improvement store. I then lined it with 1.5 inch blue foam.

My dad made me a rolling cart using a 1" thick piece of plywood and cut it to a dimension of 2 ft wide by 2.5 ft long.

He attached four study cart wheels on the base and drilled two holes in the front and threaded a piece of 3/4" diameter rope through the holes so I could pull it. Since it was flat and did not have a fold-up handle on it, it made the board light weight and fit nicely in my car trunk.

2.9 Backdrops—Buy or Make it at Home

I used an 8 ft x 8 ft blue canvas backdrop on a stand set up at jobs. This canvas size worked well with six average sized adults. When I had a large obese group of people I used a muslin backdrop which I prepared myself.

Buy a 14 ft x 14 ft painter's muslin drop cloth from any do-it-yourself store. You will also need either a bottle of navy blue or gray clothes dye. Follow the instructions on the dye bottle for dying the muslin in the washing machine.

On the top bar that went between the backdrop stands, I pinned the muslin across the top. Or if you have a sewing machine, turn over one end of the cloth and sew it together so the bar can slide through the slot.

Most drop cloths have a seam down the middle which along with the pins across the top, requires editing out. You may also have to clone in additional backdrop to cover any floor or walls that extend beyond the backdrop borders.

If you are planning upon moving into commercial studio work, there are larger sized canvas and muslin backdrops in different colors available at **Backdrop Outlet** or the **Denny Company**.

The word muslin may also sound like the word Muslim to people. One time I told a lady I was bringing my muslin backdrop and she looked at me with a surprised expression and said, *"Oh no, I don't want a religious themed backdrop, I want the blue backdrop."* It took a moment to grasp and understand what she meant. I then laughed and explained what a muslin backdrop was. She too had a good laugh.

2.10 Lighting the Portrait

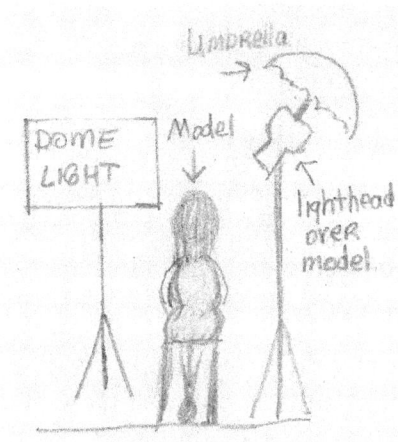

The pencil sketch here shows a standard light set up for taking portraits.

The light dome is positioned about five feet in front and to the left of the person. This is called the *main light*. Raise it up just above the person's head and position the light dome down toward the person.

L. L. Smith 2014 Light set-up illustration

Another light head and umbrella is positioned on the right above the persons head and directed down. This is called the *hair light*.

Use a light meter to meter the *main light* and note the F-stop. Next meter the *hair light* which will be about one stop less than the main light.

For example, if the *main light* meters at F/9 and the *hair*

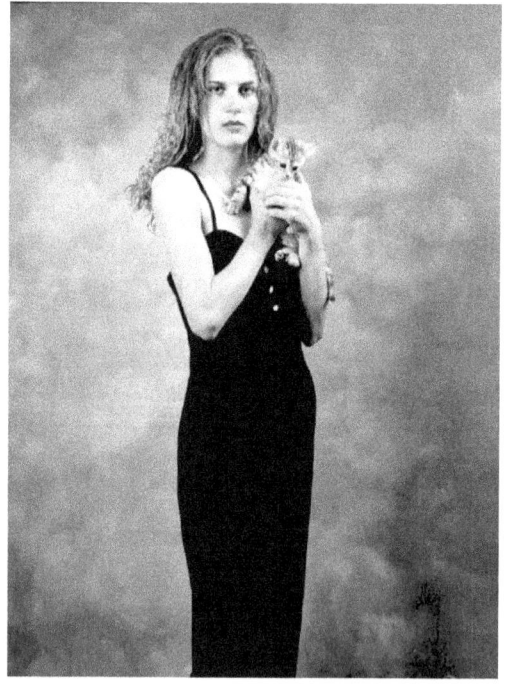

light meters at F/8, you would set the F-stop dial on your light meter for F/8.5 to balance out the light.

The photo of my daughter holding the kitten was taken using a main and hair light, plus a mini slave. Note how her hair is highlighted on the side and how the mini slave is highlighting the blue canvas behind her.

This lighting is also used for taking business portraits in your home studio. The photo of me on the right is the correct cropping for a head shot. ⟶

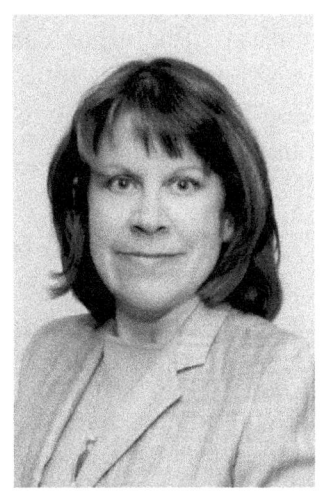

Blue photo paper can be taped onto a wall behind your subject or you can use a canvas backdrop. It is not recommended to use a muslin backdrop as it is too grainy.

When editing a head shot use the scratch remover feature in the **Paint Shop Pro** software to remove lines from around the eyes, acme, moles, and other visible blemishes from the face.

2.11 Editing Software—Affordable & Effective

I used the **Corel Paint Shop Pro** editing program to edit my photo jobs. It is easy to use and costs about $79.00. There is the option of downloading a 30 day trial version at Corel.

Since I had my digital F-stop metering down to a science, I only had to do minor lightening corrections using the One Step Photo Fix feature. My editing time took only about one minute or less per photo.

Paint Shop Pro also has other one click features that turn color photos into black & white, sepia, or adds photo borders. There is also cloning, scratch removal, layers, dodging and burning editing tools.

Plus the face smoothing, soft focus and color correcting tools means no more smearing Vaseline on or placing pantyhose over your camera lens to soften the image, let alone buying haze or polarizing filters to soften or color correct your photos.

The other editing program that photographers use is **Photoshop**. You can either pay a monthly usage fee or buy the software. Photoshop can be used for editing photo jobs—but it is not one of those pull out of the box, install and start using. You have to read the user manual to learn how to use the vast number of operations.

If you already have Photoshop 6.0 or higher on your computer, you can buy the Creative Suite upgrade for hundreds of dollars less than the full version. This upgrade, though, will not work for Photoshop Elements. Photoshop CS is also used for the **Fong Soft** flush mount album software.

Now if you are submitting images to stock sites such as Corbis or Getty, their editing guidelines are based on using **Photoshop** and **Lightroom**. The **Adobe** website offers free video tutorial on how to use lightroom.

Mystic Tint, Tone, and Color

This program is from **AutoFX** and corrects color issues, alters portrait shots, and enhances skin, hair, lips, and eyes.

I used the hand tint feature to colorize the B & W photo of me holding my long passed on cat Tommy. (Sorry the photo is still B & W.)

To try this program, at the **Auto FX** web site, you can download a 30 day trial version demo.

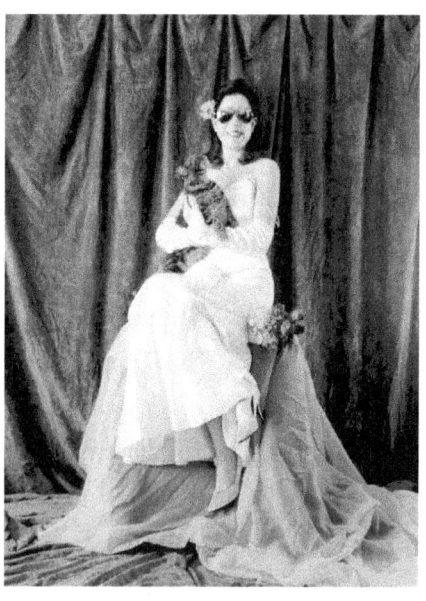

L. L. Smith 1992 Holding the cat

36

Virtual Painter 5

This program paints photos in different styles. I brought mine from Jasc, but when I did an internet search for the website, I instead found many other free download sites. However, I suggest be cautious when downloading. As my one IT acquaintance told me, *"If it's free, you end up paying me."*

Useful Tip: When you buy software, buy the physical disc instead of the download software from the products website. When you download software from a site, it is coded to embed the hard drive serial number into the software. That is why, even if you don't register the software, you automatically receive updates from the website.

Plus, that user agreement we all check, contains a clause that you can only use the software download on one computer. If want to use to install it on other computers, you have to buy another download, as the program will quit working.

And even if you make a backup disk of the download in case your computer dies, when you go to install the software into a new computer that is why…

A renewal notice pops up stating that the program is going to expire in so many days. Then you have to click on the provided link to go the website to buy a new or upgraded version.

On the other hand, this usually does not occur with a physical software disk, unless you register it. Though, some programs such as QuickBooks, has a limited support time before you have to upgrade or buy a new program.

Chapter 3 TAKING A PHOTO

3.1 Are you focused?

When using autofocus on a camera, the subject(s) has to be within the magnifying frame area in order for the photo to be in focus. For example let's say you are taking a photo of a bridal couple lighting the unity candle, and there happens to a podium to the side that is closer to the photographer than the couple is.

The AF points and the dots around the magnifying frame will focus in on the closer object which is the podium. The bridal couple will then be out of focus.

The way to correct this is to center the bride and groom in the middle of the magnifying frame, push your finger lightly down on the shutter button to focus. Then without taking your finger off the shutter, move the camera to center the scene and take the photo. Or zoom in on the bride and groom to focus which makes them the closest item to the magnifying frame.

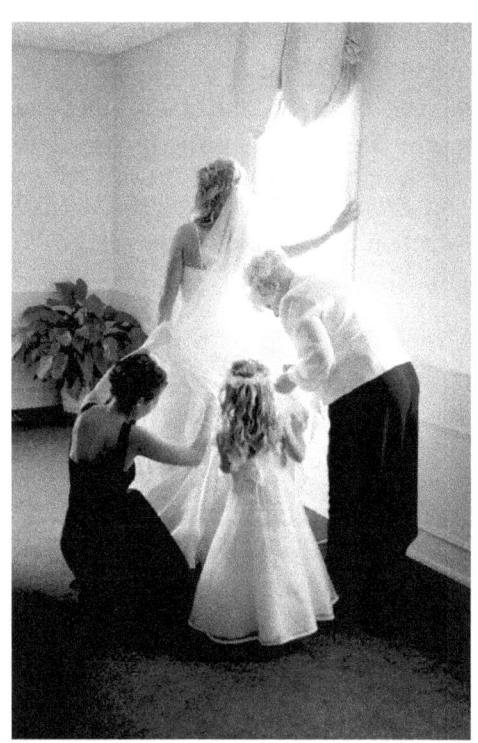

L. L. Smith 2008 Pampering the Bride

When using auto-metering with existing or ambient light without flash in a wide angle shot, the lens will meter on the lightest item such as a wedding dress. The aperture opening will be smaller and the photo will be on the darker side.

But unlike the colors that wash out on an over exposed digital image when edited, this doesn't happen with a darker image.

Instead meter manually on a color closest to gray, such as the skin, and take the photo.

For example in the photo of the bride on previous page, I had walked into the room and knew this was a great moment.

So I put my camera on manual and zoomed in on the brides bare shoulder skin for the f/stop as that is middle gray in the Zone System discussed below. I then zoomed back out, refocused and took the photo.

3.2 Easy Metering for a Wedding

When shooting outdoors with or without fill flash, set the ASA to 400 when it is cloudy and use 100 ASA for bright sunny days. It is best to manually meter your photos.

For metering outdoors in the sun, use the Zone System that was developed by Ansel Adams, whose favorite place to photograph was Yosemite Park.

The zone system is a chart that starts with the number 0 through number 10. Zero to 1 is pure black... 5 can be described subjectively as middle gray and 10 is pure white. Middle gray is items such as a gray card or wall, dirt, a light brown tree trunk, or light reflecting off the palm of your hand.

To use the Zone System metering, set the camera to manual. Then zoom in and meter using the light reflecting off the palm of your hand, or a person's face, or a gray card or wall.

When shooting photos in the shade use your external flash set as the fill flash and manually meter on a person's face. It is not recommended to use autometering, as the focal point of the lens will focus on the brightest object such as a brides white dress. This will make the lens aperture smaller which brings out the detail in the white dress but makes the rest of photo darker.

If you are using autometering and there is a dark area such as a black tux, the camera focal point will cause the aperture to open wider, washing out the facial and lighter tones.

This creates a problem during editing because the colors will lack depth and richness plus the facial tones tend to go to the red side. So I have to use the Paint Pros white balance editing feature to reduce the redness.

Another lighting situation where I need the white balance is, when white skin and blonde hair has a red tint due the diffused bounce flash hitting a brown or amber colored ceiling.

When I shot indoor flash photos with film, I could set my f/stop at 5.6 because the photo lab corrected the lighting. When I switched to digital I had to adjust the f/stops based on distance from the object or person to me to avoid flash washout of faces and light areas.

Here are the following ASA and f/stop settings with bounce flash and the Gary Fong Whale Tail.

ASA 800, F/4—Wide angle room shot from a corner

ASA 800, F/5.6
- In a church with high ceilings of the processional and or recessional
- Wide angle dancing photos of guests from a distance on a chair

ASA 400, F/8
- The garter and bouquet toss
- In a hall with high ceilings with the couple cutting the cake or dancing at distance
- Full wide angle table shots of guests

ASA 400, F/10—Close-up face shots of couples dancing

ASA 400, F/11—Wide angle of the cake and gift tables from 5.5 to 6.0 ft away

Other settings
- Close up photos of people during a ceremony: **ASA 400, f/8 to f/11**

- Close up photos of the wedding cake with ten foot ceilings: **ASA 800, f/18 to f/22** to avoid white icing washout and losing the design definitions.

3.3 Get Those Photos at Eye Level

We all have at one time or another seen this situation at family gatherings and social events, the amateur photographer running about and interrupting peoples conversations to take a picture or hanging over a baby and telling them to look up.

Not only is this inconsiderate and uncomfortable, but also can be annoying.

But you are not an amateur, you are a professional that asks permission to take photos. Plus, you get down to eye level so babies and people don't have to stretch their necks to look up at you.

Babies and children

You should have your camera ready by having it on and in your hand. A spontaneous cute moment is measured in seconds, not minutes, while you run to grab the camera, turn it on, and then try to pose the baby or tell kids to again redo the cute thing you saw.

Do this a few times and you will have crying babies every time you come near them and kids running the other way.

Baby's necks do not have the strength to keep looking up at you as you hover over them and keep saying "Hey baby, look up here." Instead you need to get down to a babies and child's eye level. Even if means lying down on the carpet or in the grass flat on your stomach.

And since babies are not adults, let them move. If the baby wants to crawl, crawl with them. When wanting a baby to sit still, find a way to keep them occupied or otherwise the baby will become frustrated, fussy, and cry.

A toddler's attention span is about five seconds, so don't expect them to sit still while you fiddle with metering and focusing your camera. You may have to play with the child and definitely speak in soft tones to keep the child from crying and running back to mom.

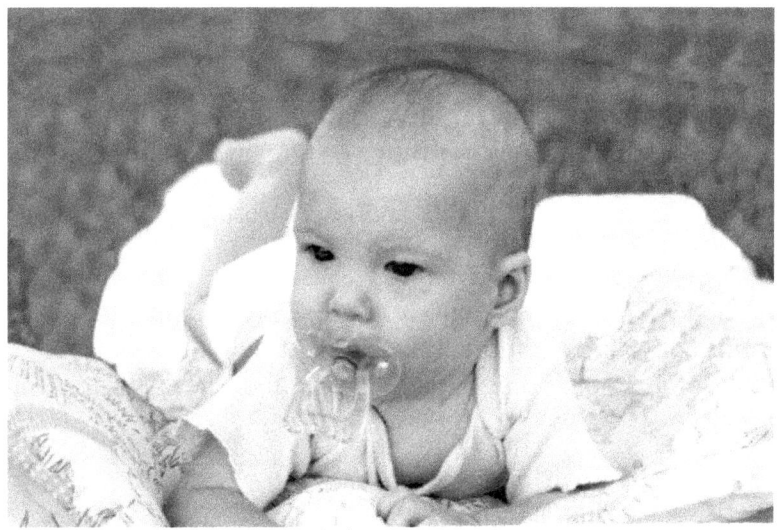

Photo L. L. Smith 1982 Baby on Blanket

The one way I got the babies, toddlers and young children's attention was to make goofy noises such as meowing, barking, and grunting pig sounds. This might not sound professional, but it worked and not only had the babies and children laughing, but the adults too.

At a wedding when photographing a large group of people with small children I would do kind of whooping sound. I usually had to remind the people holding the children to look at me and not the child.

3.4 Filling the Frame & Posing People

Are you aware that our minds are programmed to fill in blank spaces? That is why people hang photos, posters, shelves, clocks, and other items onto blank walls. This is also why when a child is coloring on a white sheet of paper with crayons, he or she fills in the entire sheet with the subject matter, sky, and grass.

That is why when an amateur photographer takes a photo of a person surrounded by scenery, the person in the photo ends up lost in the scene. This is because the surroundings satisfied the need our brain has to fill in blank areas.

Filling in the frame with the subject is one of *"those secrets"* that differentiate the amateur photographer from a professional.

When I taught a person how to frame an object—I placed a lamp against a white wall and opened the lens to wide angle. I then had the person look through the view finder and told them to focus in on the lamp. I noted that along with focusing,

the person would start zooming in the lens to fill in the blank area around the lamp.

When I took the camera and looked at their focusing in the viewfinder—the lamp filled about half of the frame. I then zoomed in the lamp, just leaving a narrow blank space around the lamp outline.

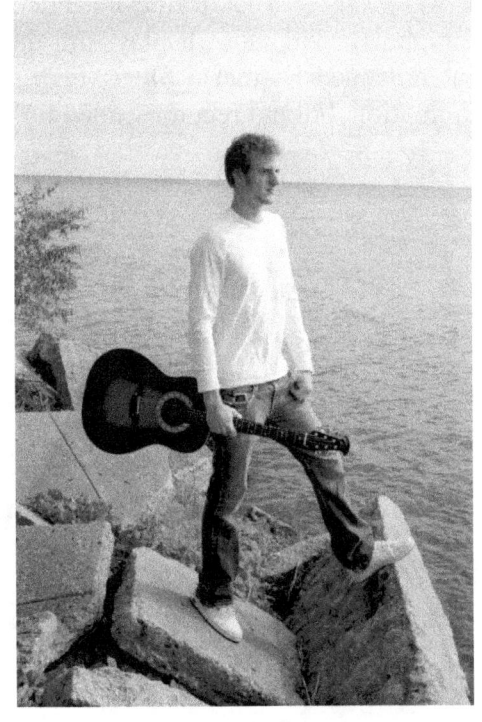

I then handed the camera back to the person and when they looked through the viewfinder, they moved their head back while saying "wow, that's close".

The reason that the person was now moving their head back was because the lamp was invading their personal space. Hence, it will take practice looking at zoomed in objects through the viewfinder to condition the mind to fill the frame.

Along with filling in the frame, is learning to crop in the lens when shooting. Cropping in the lens will prevent the urge to crop those "vast space around the person" photos during the editing process.

When cropping original photos for enlargements, make sure when saving the cropped image to click on "save as" instead of just "save." Then rename the cropped photo which will preserve the original photo.

Save your images as a JPEG when posting them on a website. Formats such as PSD (Photoshop), DNG (digital negatives) TIFF (Target file format), and PNG (portable Network Graphics) will not display on the web. A GIF (graphic interchange Format) file works for web graphics and animation, but not recommended for photos.

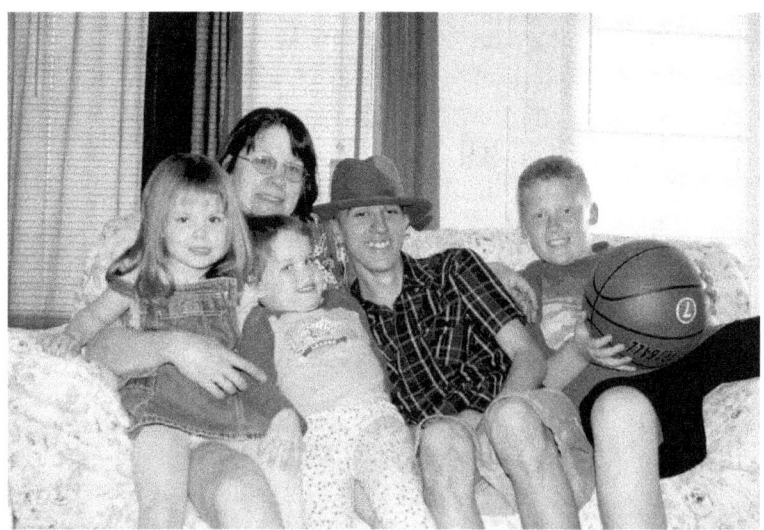

Puckett, E. A. 2011 Family photo 1

Also you need to crop in the lens when shooting so when making 5" x 7", 8" x 10"s, 11" x 14"s from the original photo, there will be enough space around your subject to avoid the cutting off body parts.

The before photo on the previous page of my grandkids and I sitting on the couch was taken by my daughter.[7] The cropping in the lens was just a little too tight on the sides. Hence when the after photo below was cropped to an 8" x 10" my granddaughter and grandson's hands were cut off.[8]

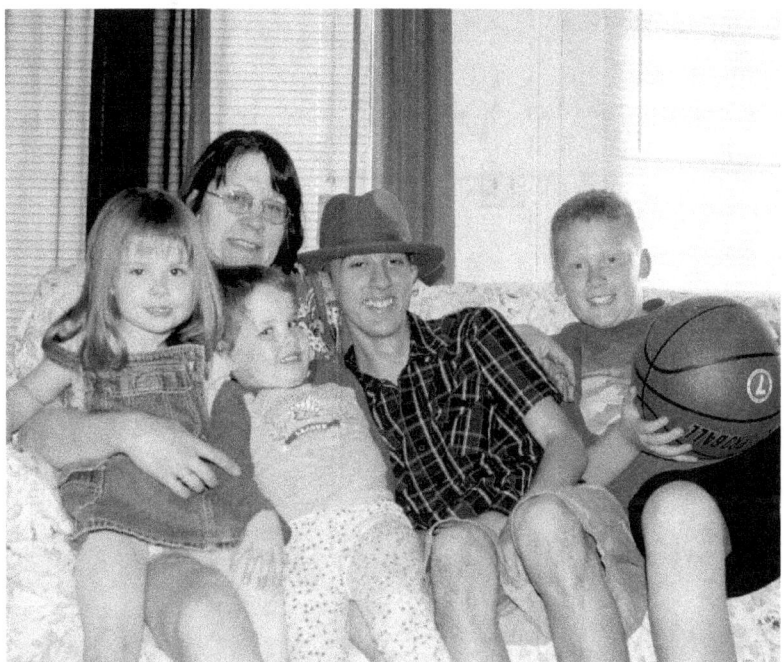

Puckett, E. A. 2011 Family photo 2

Plus another "pro tip" my daughter should have used was to avoid cutting off the knees right below the joints.

Another photography technique that sets the pro apart from the amateur is learning to turn the camera vertical when the subject(s) is vertical. This takes practice as the mind is conditioned to shoot everything in a horizontal format which results in the tops of people heads, tall buildings, and trees, to be cut off or compressed and tiny. You will note the two vertical photos of the man with the guitar and by the tree.

To have people keeping their eyes open and smiling before taking a photo it helps to say, "Okay, one, two, three, smile, DON'T BLINK."

When taking wide angle photos of a group where people are sitting on a couch—have the people all move to the edge, sit up straight, turn sideways, and tuck their feet under them. Have the people place their hands in the lap close to their body.

The reason for this is that feet and hands will stand out in a photo and appear large.

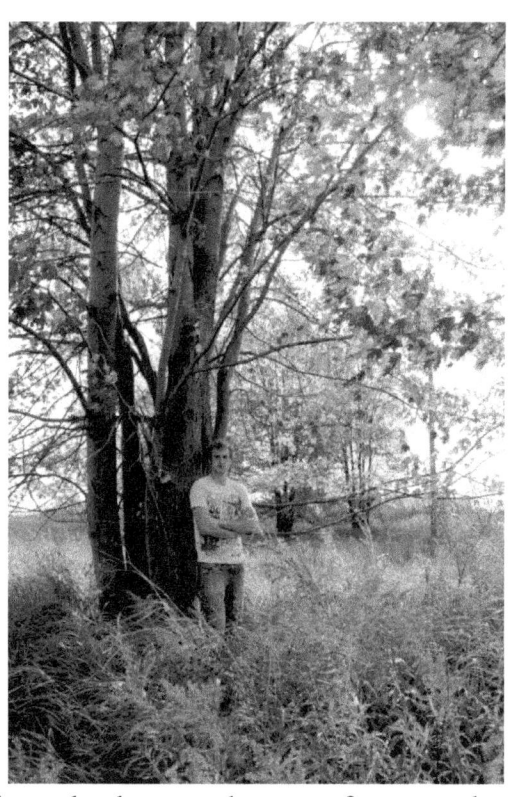

If people are standing up behind the couch have the group turn sideways in the same direction that the people on the couch are sitting.

Have a person sit on each couch arm to fill in the empty space at the end.

If you are taking a wide angle photo or close up of a person by a tree or other stationary object put the person on the side and not in the middle. Note the man by the tree in the photo.

Dealing with the Pets

With pet photography one has to love animals as they can sense our emotional state. Also unlike people, when taking a photo it is best to maintain a distance of least five to six feet to avoid appearing confrontational.

If you are at an event where people are bringing in their pets, it is best to stay in the same spot to take the photos while the pet or family is being positioned.

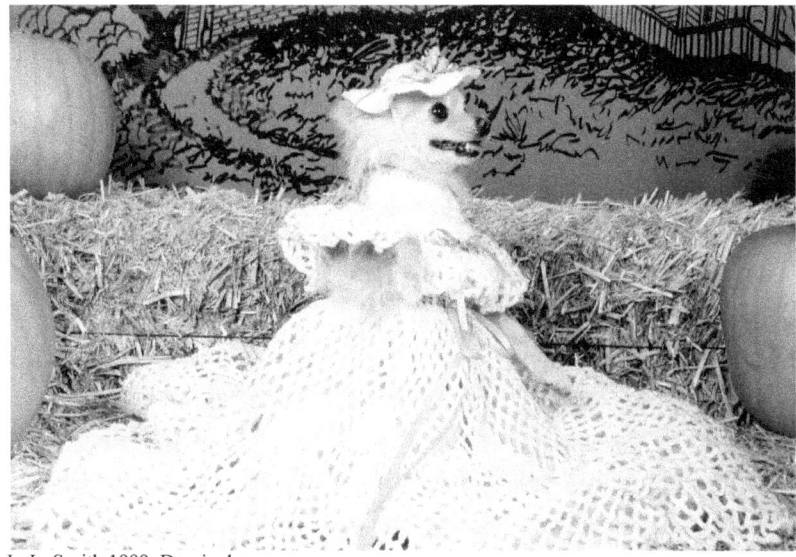

L. L. Smith 1999 Dog in dress

When you are ready to take the photo, put the camera up to your face to cover your eyes to avoid appearing confrontational. To get the pets attention says the pets name in sing song voice. The owner will probably stand behind you to help attract the dogs' attention. It is a group effort.

The dog photo above was taken at a pet rescue organization photo shoot. The members paid $7.50 for 2—5" x 7"s and I received half of the money. The organization provided the backdrop and props. It was a three hour event and I made $487.50 plus $175.00 from reprints and enlargements. I also did their Santa paws event which was pet photos with Santa. I made about the same amount of money.

3.5 JPEG vs. RAW

At a wedding it is not uncommon to shoot upwards of 350 to 400 images. For that reason JPEG is the preferred mode as it processes the images as they are shot. JPEG mode is also readable by any editing program on the market, and by the

Microsoft Office Picture Manager, and Windows Picture Viewer programs on a computer.

A JPEG image is compressed and the file size is smaller than a RAW file. An 8 megapixel camera will produce a JPEG between 1 and 3 MB's in size. The JPEG is also higher in contrast and sharper.

And since the image is processed in the camera as you take the photo, it is immediately usable for printing, sharing, or posting on the Internet or other media sites. Plus, you can edit the image without losing data each time.

In contrast when shooting in the RAW mode, images are not processed by the camera. They have to be downloaded onto the computer to be edited. The software program often used for editing RAW images is Photoshop. Unfortunately, when editing, data is lost with each edit process step.

Also when shooting in the RAW mode the image is uncompressed. If you using a 20 megapixel camera, it will produce an 18 MB raw file. This lowers the images contrast, making it flatter, washed out and not as sharp.

Shooting in the RAW mode is often used for editing images for commercial use and for submission to stock photography sites.

Chapter 4 LIGHTING THE SCENE

4.1 Different Types of Lighting

The following are the four types of lighting techniques used to create exciting and beautiful photographs.

Ambient light is known as existing light which can be incoming window sunlight, incandescent lamps, candles or other lighting. Incandescent lighting gives color photos a yellow hue which can be avoided by adjusting the white balance on your camera, using fill flash or the Paint Shop Pro white balance editing tool.[9]

Renaissance lighting is light coming in from above such as through ceiling windows, or the light from the bounce flash on the camera.[9]

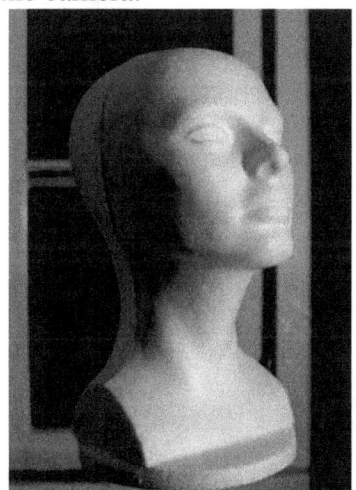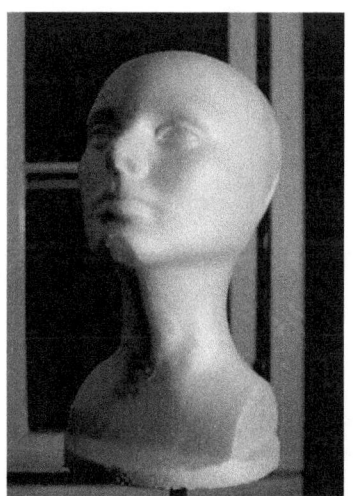
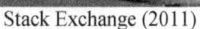
Stack Exchange (2011)

Broad lighting (left image) is when the main light is directed onto the side of the face that is closest to the camera. Broad lighting adds roundness or thickness to the face and is best used for a thin face. Avoid this with larger or heavier subjects and those with fuller faces.[9]

Short lighting (right image) is when the main light is directed at the side of the face that is furthest away from the camera.

49

This should be used for people with a thin face or a person who is heavy, or with a rounder faces.[9]

4.2 Outdoor lighting techniques

A scrim is a type of filter used to soften sunlight, eliminate shadows on the face, and distribute light evenly. Scrims are used in movie scenes to diffuse the harsh and bright sunlight. That is why the actors look like they are in the shade.

Clouds are a natural scrim filter which is ideal for shooting outdoor photos with fill flash. On sunny days, you can make a scrim by clamping a white sheet onto the pole between two light stands, or suspend the sheet over a rope between two trees, or have people hold up the sheet.

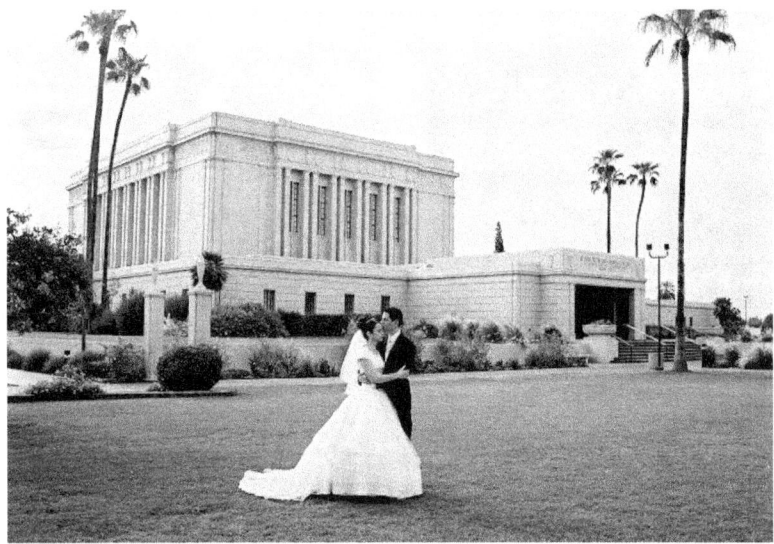

L. L. Smith 1999 Couple by Mormon Temple AZ

In both the summer and winter time when the sun is directly overhead, avoid taking photos as it washes out the colors and casts harsh shadows on people's faces. Harsh shadows can make a person look five years older. Best option is to take photos in the shade with fill flash.

The photo above was taken at the Mormon Temple in Mesa Arizona on a rare cloudy and cool summer day. I was always being hired by couples to take photos midday during the hot summer time outside after a temple wedding. Even after the couple saw my portfolio midday photos with shadows on faces, they still wanted photos taken at noon. It was miserable being outside in the 115 degree heat. I had to bring paper towels to blot away the sweat off theirs and my face.

In the morning when the sun is at a 45 degree angle the light saturates and brightens the colors. Hence, take the winter time morning photos between 9:00 a.m. to 11:00 a.m. In the summer time take photos between 7:00 a.m. to 9:00 a.m.

The best times to take photos in the summer time is between 6:30 p.m. to 8:30 p.m. as the afternoon sun warms the skin tones and enriches the colors. Take the winter time afternoon photos between 2:30 p.m. to 4:30 p.m.

4.3 How to light up a Model

The next two outdoor lighting methods are used by commercial photographers when they shoot photos for swimsuit magazines and sportswear catalogues. The equipment used is white or golden fill cards, scrims, and light colored walls.

Sunlight is reflected off the fill cards to light up the models face and create a hair light at the same time. Light is also filtered through the scrim, or reflected off a light colored wall onto the model.

Fill cards can be either white or golden toned and made of foam, poster, or photo mount board material. The measurements are 2 ft wide x 2.5 ft long. A scrim can be a white sheet, or thin white material, or architectural tracing paper. The size depends upon the area to be covered.

The first lighting method is using a wall. The photographer stands with their back against the wall facing the model. The model should be positioned about six feet in front of the photographer for the face shot. Have the model move further back for fuller body shots.

I took the 1990 photo of my daughter below with Fuji 100 ISO ASA slide film in my 35 mm Canon AE1 film camera. It was taken in front of a white brick wall in the backyard of the house I was living in at the time. It was about 4:30 p.m. in the winter time. I metered manually using my daughters face as middle gray.

The f/stop was at f/8 with an 80 shutter speed. Despite the small aperture opening and a somewhat fast shutter speed, the background is still out of focus due to the focal points in the lens being centered on my daughters face.

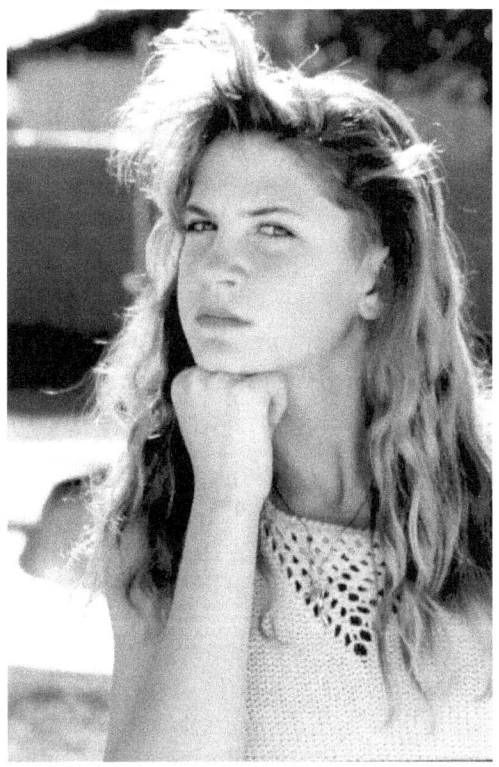

When shooting with slide film, it has to be bracketed at different camera shutter speeds. Bracket at 50, 60, 80, and 125 shutter speeds at f/8, using the fill card set up described on the next page.

Even though the shutter speed is 60 for a Canon Camera when using film, the shutter speed for slide film was 80.

Before digital commercial photographers shot with 35 mm, 120, 220, and 4 x 5 slide films and placed their slides into heavy cardboard portfolio slide holders. The holders were 11" x 14" with 32 openings and had a clear heavy plastic sleeve to protect the slides.

When a photographer met with the client—the holder was laid on top of a light table to view the slides. The photographer usually shot with either a medium format or a 4 x 5 camera that had a pricy Polaroid back they attached to the back of the camera. Then the photographer would take a test shot of the product set up for the art director to look at—to make sure it was lighted correctly before shooting with the slide film.

Digital has definitely contributed to the cost savings for the commercial photographer.

The light coming off of a white wall is harsh and can cause your models eyes to tear. To avoid that have your model close their eyes until you are ready to take the photo.

The next outdoor lighting method as shown in the drawing requires the use of white or golden fill cards and two people to hold the cards. Golden fill cards are used to give skin a richer tone.

The best time to take photos is in the morning when the sun is at a 45^0 angle.

The two fill card holders turn the cards in and towards the model leaving about a 1.5 ft gap between the cards. ⟶

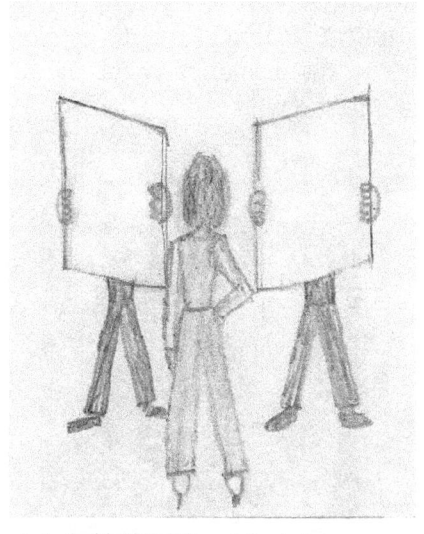

The model faces the cards with the sun behind her. The light reflects off the cards onto the model.

L. L. Smith 2014 Fill card illustration

The photographer then positions themselves on the other side of the opening between the fill cards. Next they fill the frame, manually meter, refocus on the models face, and shoot.

As with the white wall set up, the sunlight that is reflecting off the fill cards may cause the model to tear up. Have her close her eyes until you are ready to take the photo.

Window Light

Using window lighting without fill flash gives photos a sense of depth. In this photo I manually metered on my nieces face to set the F/stop.

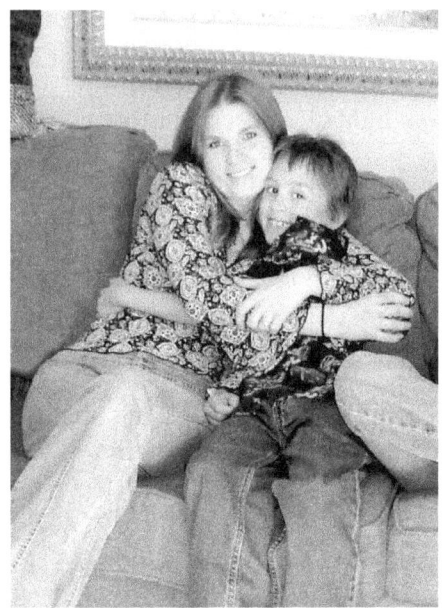

When using the auto-metering on a camera, turn off the flash unit to prevent the camera flash from popping up and firing which flattens the image.

If a person is next to a window, first photo below, meter manually on the face, crop in, and take the photo next to the wall .

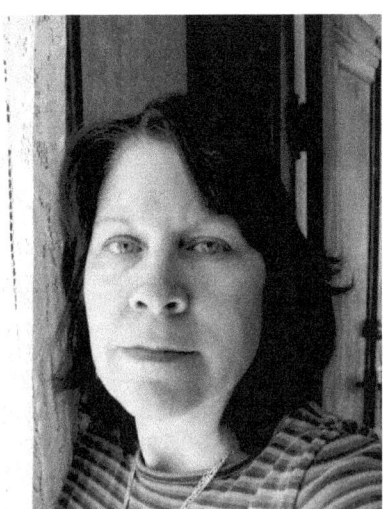
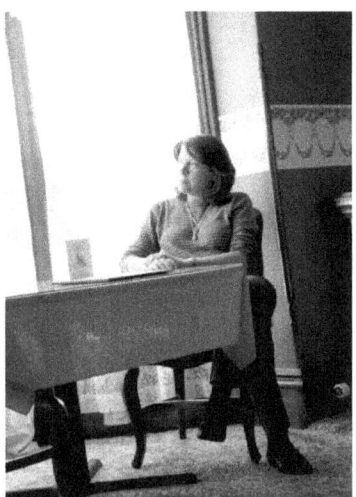

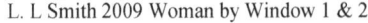
L. L Smith 2009 Woman by Window 1 & 2

When taking a wide angel view photo of a room with light coming in through the curtains, use fill light to balance out the light in the middle of the room. The second photo of the woman sitting in the chair was taken with no fill flash and as a result the curtains are washed out.

When taking a photo of a hotel room, use studio lights for either open or closed curtain photos. This is will balance out the light throughout the room and will show the outside scenery also.

4.4 The Observation Deck—Are You Looking?

One technique that sets the professional photographer apart from an amateur is keen observation of their surroundings.

When photographing any event, scan the environment constantly for unique, humorous, or romantic moments. The eyes should also do a quick "through the viewfinder" scan of the surroundings before taking the photo.

It will take practice to become proficient and quick at "through the viewfinder" scanning. But once this technique is mastered, it helps prevent your photos from containing the following faux pas:

- Items like EXIT signs, plaques, clocks, or shelves on walls above the heads of people or

- Telephone poles, tree branches, lamp posts and other items sticking out of a person's body or

- Chairs, tables, items on tables, microphone stands and podiums in a photo or

- Crooked ties and collars, glare on eye glasses, messy hair or sunglasses on people indoors or

- Open jackets or trouser zippers or

- Purses in women's hands

At wedding receptions after taking the photo of the smiling bridal couple being served at the start of the buffet line, set down your camera and fall into line behind the family to get your food. And don't be concerned about offending anyone because you need to be done eating in time to start taking photos of the bridal couple visiting the guest tables.

During the meal, still glance around to see what is going on. If there is an open seat next to you, set your camera on the chair. Or if not, place the camera where you can reach it if you need to take a photo.

Being discrete during a photography job should be exercised at all times. People like when the photographer is quick with a click of the camera and out of there.

For example, during the bridal couple's first dance, approach the couple, and say, "Look this way" then focus, snap the photo and move away. Then take the rest of the photos from a distance. The same applies with the father/daughter and mother/son dances.

You know you are doing your job well, when your clients are surprised and excited to see that special moment photo they did not know happened. Plus, they will compliment you on how nonintrusive and patient you were.

Patience is a virtue and will be tested when encountering the inconsiderate person who wanders off when it's time for photos. Stay patient and keep working, the bridal couple or other family members will take care of the situation.

Also, when meeting the soon-to-be bride, be wary of them asking too many questions about refunds if they don't like the pictures. I had a few of those.

The problems always started when the bride came to get her photos after the wedding. She would quickly look at the photos and not say anything. Then paid and left.

About two weeks later, I would get a call from the bride wanting a partial refund, because she did not like some of the photos.

I then stated "I'm sorry to hear that. But you didn't say anything at the time when you were looking at the photos. Plus you paid me and left. And according to the agreement form you signed, once you examine the photos, pay, and leave the premises, there are no refunds."

The bride would argue with me and I would restate my position. Eventually, when she realized I was not going to refund any monies back to her, she ended the call.

I also had a bride one time who wanted a refund because she had told me she did not want any photos with people smoking in them. After she came and got the photos she called me a week later screaming at me that I had ruined one of the most important photos. She claimed I had purposely taken a photo of her bridesmaids smoking in the photo. I asked her which photo and I pulled it up on my computer.

It was an impromptu photo of the bride with a group of her coworkers after the outdoor formal photo session. Other people were milling about in the background. Then I saw two bridesmaids who were out of focus smoking in the distance.

I said, "You didn't say anything at the time about the two bridesmaids smoking in the background, or you would have had moved everyone to another spot." She continued to still blame me and then threatened to sue me.

Finally, I said "Okay, you go ahead and go to court to prove you deserve a refund. And if you win, it won't even cover the $175.00 filing fee, the $50.00 process server fee, the pay you will lose taking time off work and paying a babysitter. Good bye." And I hung up.

Amazingly, I never heard another word from her.

Bottom line: Observe the prospective clients behavior. If you feel uncomfortable, follow your instincts and pass on the job.

Chapter 5 MORE PHOTO TIPS

5.1 Stock Photography

As a photographer you may already know about stock photography sites. If you do a stock photography Google search, it comes back with over 128,000,000 web results. This chapter will focus on eight of the more popular sites.

Stock photography can generate income if you know the right type of photos to submit to the premium stock sites. It is not the lazy mans way to photography riches, as it does take time and effort to take the photos the stock sites are looking for... have the model releases signed... edit the photos according to the stock site submission requirements... and then submit to the review boards to see if you will be accepted.

Plus, it is something you have to enjoy and love doing in order to be successful.

Stock photography will also require the use of that light tent from Adorama for taking table top photos of product.

Now in order to make money at stock photography you need to know what the premium stock sites, such as Corbis and Getty want from a photographer.

However, not all the stock sites will offer that information. There are sites that will let anyone register, then upload both good and poor quality images, and set pricing. Downside is, even with all the right SEO keywords, if your images are not what buyers are looking for, they are going to languish in stock site purgatory.

For example the digital image of the plated food featured on the next page was one of six I took during a wedding. The restaurant paid me $275.00 to use the images on its menus. I then uploaded the photos onto Art.com., a free site, and entered my keywords. Six months later none of the photos had sold, so I removed them.

Now had I attempted to submit those same images to a stock site like Getty Images, it would not meet the image submission guidelines as it was not shot in the RAW format and was not edited in Photoshop CS to the stock sites photo submission specifications.

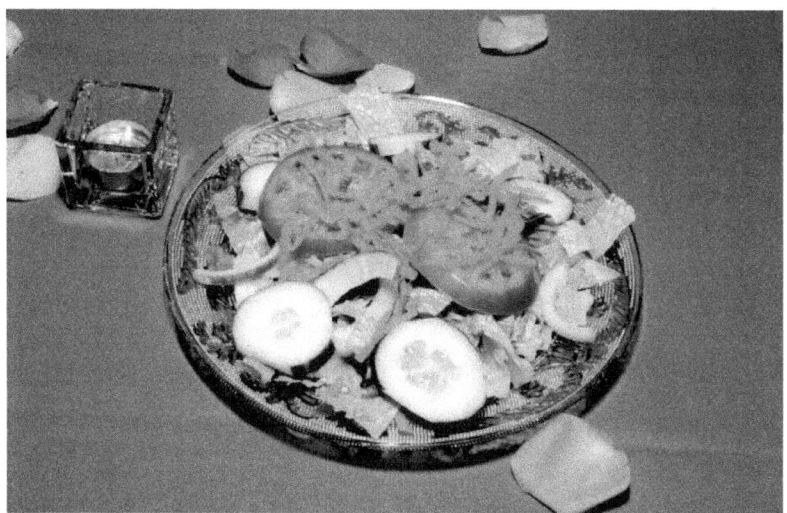

L. L. Smith 2010 Platted Food

So if you are willing to follow to the letter, a premium stock site submission guidelines, and are accepted by the review board…

Then you will be given directions on what to do so your photos will be found by the right buyers from companies and corporations with decent advertising budget. And if they buy your images, that is how you make the money.

The first thing to do is to visit one of the premium stocks sites to look at the quality of photos. When you see them you may ask yourself "can I take the same quality of photos?".

Guess what, you can, by using the photo and lighting techniques that are discussed in this guide and following the stock sites submissions. Plus, at the **iStock.com** website, there are tutorials, complete with photos on the type of images this site wants.

The Stock Sites

Art.com and **Artist Rising:** This is a freebee sites with over 64,000 members with over 358,311 images. Their unique selling point (USP) is, they give you a platform to show and sell your art or photographs as well as connect with a global community of artists. And because it is free and easy to join and upload images that is why there are 358,311 images.

There is an upgrade plan, and it might improve your chances of selling images, but I have never enrolled.

Shutterstock: This site serves customers from 150 countries with over 350 million paid downloads. You type in your email to download their free Contributor Success Guide

Fotolia: This site has over 28 million images and is based in another country and states: *"You can join our community of over 4,772,463 design and communications professionals."*

Alamy: A free site to upload images. It has over 46 million images. There is a page that explains how buyers find images through their SEO and keyword rankings.

Veer: This is a division of Corbis and after registering you submit ten of your best images for review.

Bigstock Photo: This site has a review board, over 17 million images and vectors and you have to sign up to download the submission guidelines.

Getty Images: This site has a review board and submission requirements. Here is an excerpt from the Getty Images web site of its technical requirements: *"To successfully submit your images to us for review take a look at the following technical requirements:*

- Images should be relevant to a creative, commercial stock photography collection–so subjects like news events, product photography, etc should not be included.

- Any images featuring recognizable people **require model releases**. That includes celebrities, sports figures, politicians, etc. The only exception is where we define images as being suitable for the editorial travel market, but this doesn't include street photography or editorial work.

- Private property or copyrighted artworks require a property release. That includes offices, stores, private homes, paintings, photos, sculpture and other artwork, unless you can get a release from the owner or creator.

- For 35mm digital capture, we strongly recommend use of a professional-quality digital SLR using RAW or uncompressed TIFF format. Most compact "point-and-shoot" and consumer-level cameras do not produce images of the level of quality our customers demand, and would not be suitable for submission".[10]

CORBIS Images: This site has a review board with a clear mission statement:
"Our collections are carefully chosen, and our contributors are hand-picked by editors and art directors who understand the value and currency of ideas."[11]

The review process includes a submission requirements page on why they want images edited by Photoshop:

"A custom Photoshop script catches potential image problems undetected by the Gateway upload. It reports on the number of layers and channels, bit-depth, color mode, and white and black points in a single or group of images. Please note that this is a reporting tool, not a repair tool. We recommend that you use this script as an added check of your hi-res media prior to upload. Installation instructions are provided in the ZIP file." [12]

Corbis also has a PDF with instructions for Photoshop 6, 7, and CS color setting submission requirements for changing CMYK settings to Sheetfed Coated v2 and preserving embedded profiles.

5.2 Restoring the Past

In 1990 I was so excited to be hired for my first on-location portrait session. The family wanted photos taken by the fireplace that had reflective tile on the wall above the fireplace mantle. I sat up my dome light, shot 12 photos, and took the 24 exposure roll to the lab. A week later I picked up my prints and freaked out when I saw the dome light reflection in the tile.

I consulted with the labs photo editor explaining I needed the light reflection removed out of the negatives. When he quoted me $500.00 to do the six negatives, I was aghast and passed on the retouching. I called the lady, explained what occurred and she agreed to let me retake the photos in another area of the house.

Today digital has changed the editing business. That $500.00 quote to take out a light reflection from tile, can now be done on any of the countless free photo-editing websites. Here are the top six Google searches:

- **134lunapic.com**
- **Fotoflexer.com**
- **Pixlr.com**
- **Picmonkey.com**
- **fotor.com**
- **ribbet.com**

Now if you do happen to have Photoshop CS and are proficient using it, you can still make money doing more complicated photo editing.

I found this website **Tucia.com** that will give you an idea of the cost. You buy points, at $8.00 each, depending upon what level of editing you need and amount of work required.
Even if you don't have Photoshop, the Corel Paint Shop Pro program has many of the same tools, only easier to use.

For photo restoration of old hard copy photos—it requires a negative and slide scanner. The scanned photo shown of my family on the next page from 1982—had a yellow stain in the lower right hand corner, was faded, torn, and scratched.

Most scanners have a default setting of 200 dpi (dots per square inch) which is sufficient for posting your photos on your web site portfolio. However, it is too low of a resolution for printing out hard copy photos.

A low dpi resolution file when printed into a hardcopy print will have blotchy areas of blended wavy dots. The resolution of the digital image should be at least 1 MB to avoid the wavy dots. Use the advanced settings and set the dpi to 600 which translates to between a 3 to 4 MB file for each photo.

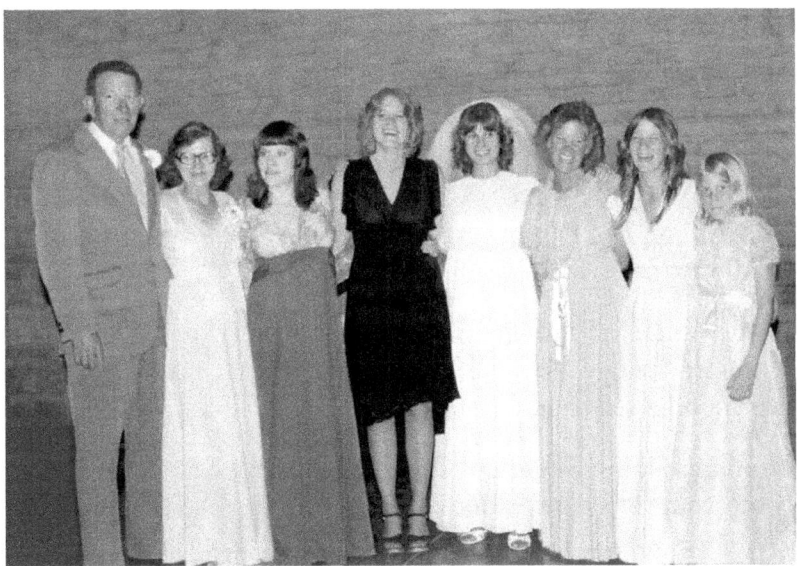

L. L. Smith 1980 Family photo restored

5.3 Photo Contests

It is easy to be lured into entering national or worldwide photo contests. The promises of high cash awards, cameras, and trips offered can make any photographer salivate and think that they have what it takes.

Back in the 1990's I entered and paid out hundreds of dollars in photo contest entry fees, but never won anything. So I quit wasting my money and instead focused on the local free or low cost juried competitions. This resulted in my winning ribbons, awards, having my photos published, and my artwork exhibited in art galleries.

Plus it was gave me exposure in the community, free advertising and material for my media website page.

But don't let my non-winning photo contest experiences stop you from entering contests. Everyone has his or her own artistic style and your photo may be the one that wins.

I have listed some of the more popular contests that are geared for the professional photographer:

Photo District News (pdnonline.com) offers a variety of different contests with prizes such as monetary gift cards, a VIP Expo Pass to a PDN photo expo, gift certificates, DSLR cameras, PDN photo serve portfolios plus a One-year subscription to PDN. Average entry fee: $45.00 single photo, $60.00 for a series.

Professional Photographers of America (PPA.com) Average entry fee, $95.00 for PPA members and non-members, $65 additional. Too steep a fee for my liking.

Photographers Forum (pfmagazine.com) has a $5.95 per photo entry fee. They offer 1st, 2nd, & 3rd place cash awards. 1st place wins an additional prize. All entrants receive two issues of Photographers Forum magazine. Proof sheets are available to buy of the page your photo appears on in their hardcopy book of the finalists and winners.

National Geographic Travel—Has a yearly contest and average entry fee is $15.00 per photo. Prizes of cash, trips, and gift certificates awarded.

Nikon Photo contest—has has been doing this contest since 1969. No entry fee and awards are cash and cameras.

World Press Photo.org—This is for photojournalists and offers cash and cameras as prizes.

5.4 How to Light up Your Product Shots

Food

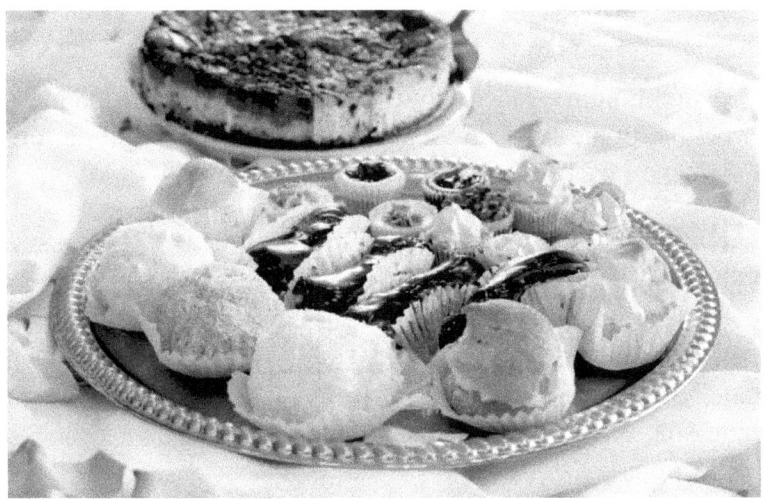

L. L. Smith 2009 Cakes on a plate—shot with window light

Place your light dome about 2 to 2.5 ft above the plate. Use a plain tablecloth. To emphasize one area of the plate, zoom in on the plate at a 45 degree angle and use a wide aperture such as f/5.6 and focus on the front part of the food. This will give the in focus look in front and will be out of focus towards the back of the plate.

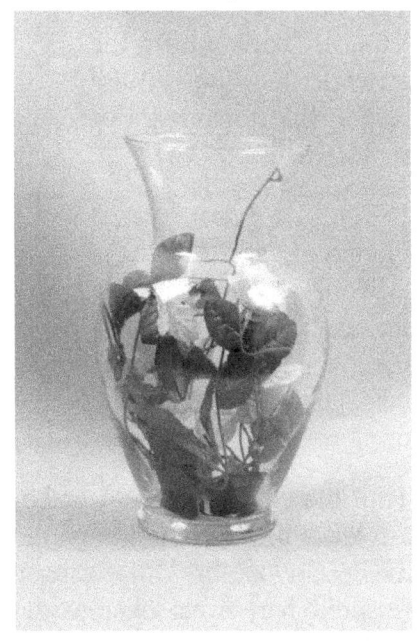

You can also use window light to give the food a more natural lighting look.

Reflective items

Photographing a glass item requires the use of two small dome lights. Place one light on one side of the glass and one on the other side. They should be about two feet away from the glass.

Using umbrellas will create round circles instead of the rectangular look on the glass.

For a dome light, place it about three feet in front of the glass. Direct the dome light down at a 45^0 angle. The resulting look is shown on the previous page of the glass vase.

Artwork

When photographing artwork, it is best to shoot in a room that is evenly lighted up by existing window light. Photographing artwork still in the glass frame or out straight on using studio lights leaves a reflection.

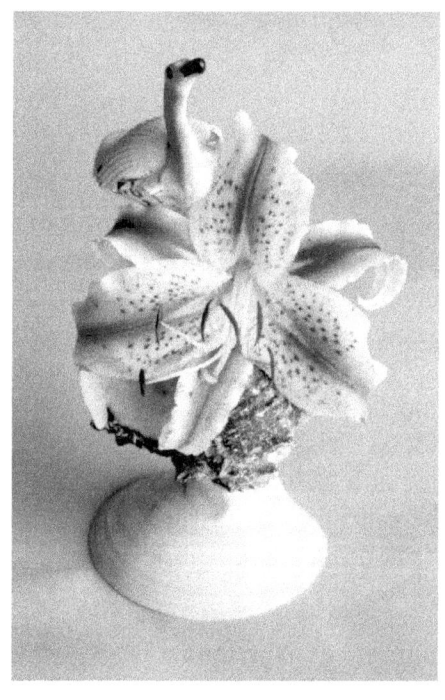

It is recommended to have the owner take their paintings out of frame. This is because if you damage or mar the artwork, you are responsible for repairs or replacement.

Use a professional mounting easel to set the artwork on. Do not tape the artwork to a wall as the tape can cause damage to the back of the print.

L. Smith Iris and Swan 2006

Turn the camera vertical or horizontal to fit the shape of the artwork. Fill the frame with the artwork, focus, manually meter, do not use fill flash and take the photo. The photo featured here was taken with window light on blue photo background paper.

5.5 Fireworks

1. It is best to use a 35 mm digital camera with RAW capacity, not a P & S.

2. Use a tripod when photographing fireworks from a distance or close-up.

3. For best results use an ASA setting of 100 to achieve optimum sharpness.

4. When photographing directly under fireworks that are bursting, place the dial setting on the no flash setting if using auto-metering.

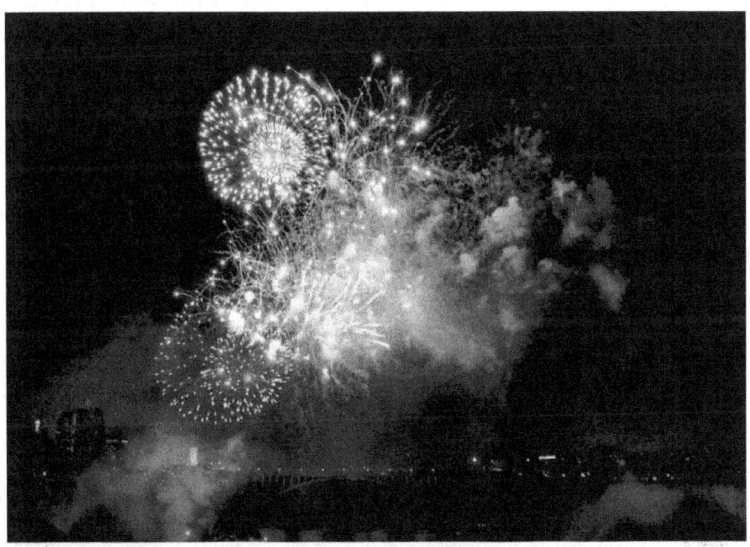

L. L. Smith 2005 Fireworks over Niagara

5. Use the manual camera settings and a remote to trigger the shutter to avoid touching the camera. You can also use the bulb setting for a series of fireworks going off—but have a piece of black paper to put up in front of the lens after the fireworks are done before turning off the bulb setting.

6. If possible have foreground scenery which adds some interest to the photo. The photo of the fireworks here shows Niagara Falls and a bridge in the foreground.

5.6 Spirit Photography

Years ago at a wedding, I took a processional photo of the bride and groom coming down the aisle. When I got the photograph back there was a large white mist in the shape of person in front of the bride. When I showed the photo to the couple, the bride said with a smile "I bet that's my grandmother, she passed three weeks before the wedding."

I was happy that she was not upset. However, not all clients can be as forgiving, especially if they don't believe in spirits making an appearance on photos.

Passed on spirits roam the earth and they may show up on the prints you are giving to your clients. When the client sees the mist or orbs they may ask if your camera or flash was not working. You should reply, "I' m sorry about that but the mist and or orbs is not due to a camera malfunction but are probably spirits." The client may or may not agree.

The photo below was taken with my 35 mm digital camera while on a tour of the Antelope Slot Canyons in Arizona. This photo contains white or silver orbs which are definitely spirits.

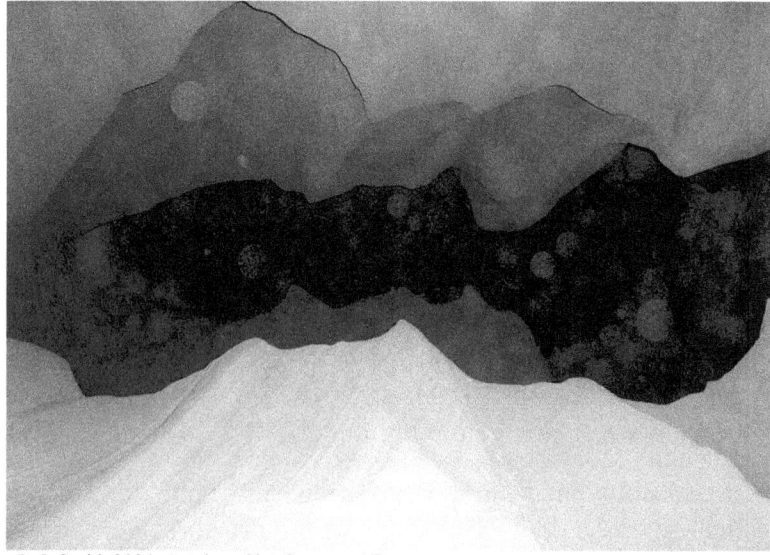

L. L Smith 2004 Antelope Slot Canyon, AZ

Here is a short description of orbs colors and meanings:

- **Clear**: They look like soap bubbles and may indicate that the entity is trying to communicate with you. This may be related to the event that occurred in that location or the spirit wants assistance to move to the other side.

- **Red or Orange**: Not related to emotion, may indicate that an entity could have been someone who during their lifetime was a caretaker over people

- **Black or Brown**: If these appear in a photo they are associated with evil, and indicate the area is an unsafe place full of negative energy. To avoid having the entity follow you home, surround oneself with a white light of love, say a prayer of protection, delete the photos, and leave the area immediately.

Years ago I attended a spirit photography presentation and the following are some highlights I learned:

- When taking spirit photography with a digital camera, use the flash.

- Tell the spirits that you mean them no harm and always thank the spirits for allowing you to take photographs.

- When visiting haunted locations don't invite spirits to be in the photographs. This is like giving permission for any entity to show up. The entity may be evil, and might attach themselves to you and those people present and follow you home. Also if you are in a location where negative energy is present, it will be more powerful during a storm and electronic equipment may not work.

5.7 Travel Photography

Here is the "*inside scoop*" to being paid to take a vacation. Let's say you are going to visit a resort. You call the resort and talk to the manager about how you're a photographer who will be visiting their resort and taking photos during your stay.

Offer to show the manager your photos on your laptop while you are there. If the manager buys even one of your photos then you can write off your trip.

To sell your vacation photos, you need to know what the stock photography agencies and travel magazine are accepting. And the way to find out is to go to the submission guidelines on stock and travel magazines websites.

When traveling, avoid doing the typical amateur tourist photographer mistake of snapping away at everything. Like the time I went to Hawaii, I took ten photos of pineapples in a field, but only one photo of the North Shore and one in Pearl Harbor. Talk about misplaced priorities.

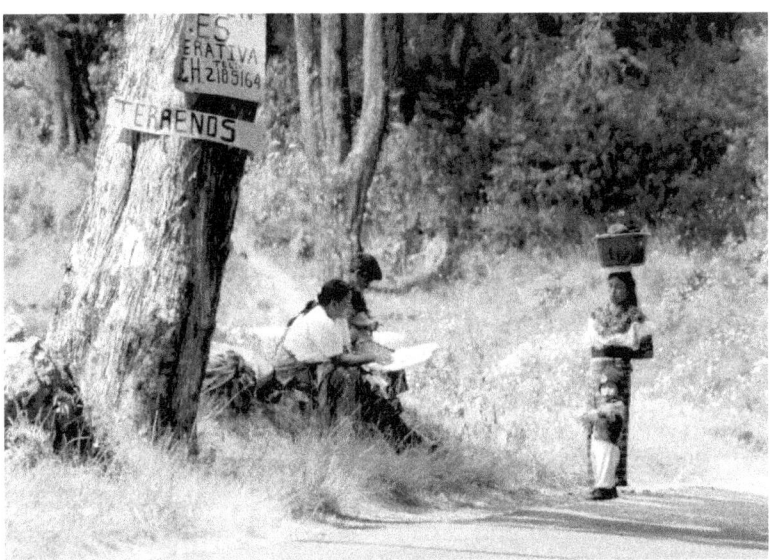

L. L. Smith 2006 People on the road in Guatemala

When you visit popular tourist destinations—remember that thousands of people have been there before you. Therefore your photos have to be different from all the other photos photographers have taken before you.

That is why outdoor photographers will hike into rough terrain, deal with wildlife, bugs, or inclement weather to get the perfect shot of something unique.

Then they sell their images on stock sites, wildlife publications, and advertising agencies.

Another way to get photos of places that are not frequented by tourists is to stay with a family in another country.

In 2006 I took a two week trip to Guatemala and stayed with a friend's family. I took over digital 600 photos using my Sigma 28-330 mm lens. The telephoto setting allowed me to take photos of people and scenery without being intrusive.

You can see a selection of my Guatemala photos at my Word Press **Clicking for Cash from Home** site.

Taking Scenery Photos

If you want to make money selling scenery photographs, they need to have that "unique attraction" and "it" factor.

As discussed previously, you have to know what art directors and publications are looking for to buy. Also you should be using the manual setting on your camera instead of the auto metering.

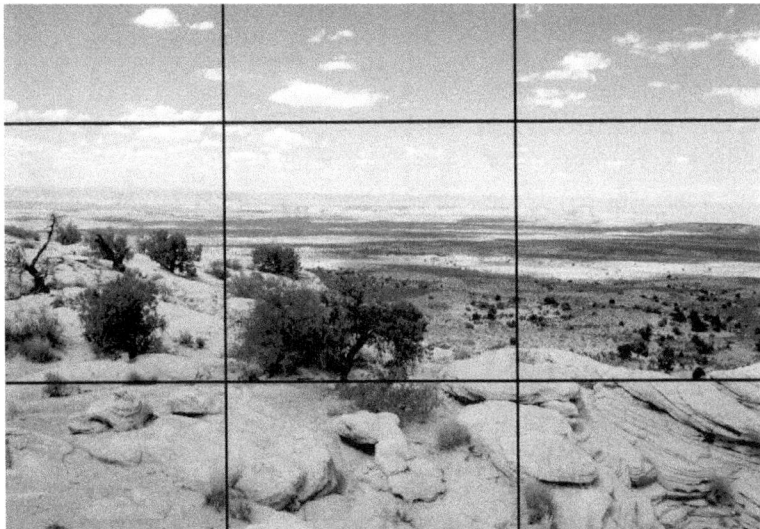

L. L Smith 2004 Northern Arizona—Rule of thirds example

Plus the image size should be set to RAW to comply with the technical editing requirements of some sites.

And if you want to be part of a photographic community that offers photographic tips written by the famous outdoor nature photographers… Plus opportunities for entering your photography for possible publication—the best one I have found is at the **National Geographic** website:

Many photographers will use a method called the rule of thirds. The idea is that you imagine breaking your image into nine different boxes both horizontally and vertically so that you have nine parts. The desert photograph featured on the previous page shows an example of what it looks like.

Next you're supposed to visualize placing the key subject matter a third of the way up, and a third of the way in from the left. This is the good area to use.

The bad places to place key items would be directly in the middle… at the top… or at the bottom or in the corner.

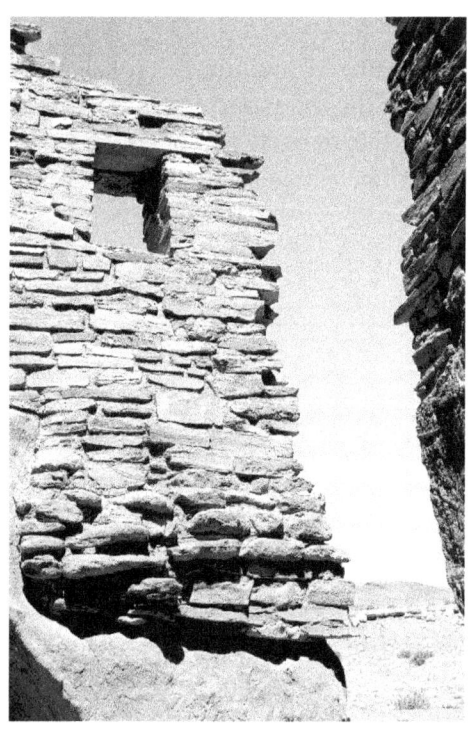

The rule of thirds can also help you overcome the tiny subject surrounded by the vast space issue explained earlier.

Another way to understand this method is too look at award winning photography you see in prominent magazines and draw lines on the photos.

L. L. Smith 2004 Wupatki

Myself, I have never used the rule of thirds as I have a natural ability to compose items in photos.

And again don't forget to turn the camera vertically and use wide angle when the scene warrants such as people standing in front of vertical buildings, trees, monuments, etc.

When I visit a park featuring Indian ruins, pyramids, unique trees, plants, insects, and wildlife, I study and look at the textures, composition, and the nooks and crannies. It is surprising what I have seen and discovered.

A good example is the photo featured in this chapter of the Wupatki Indian ruins in Arizona which show the texture of the stones and how they are layered.

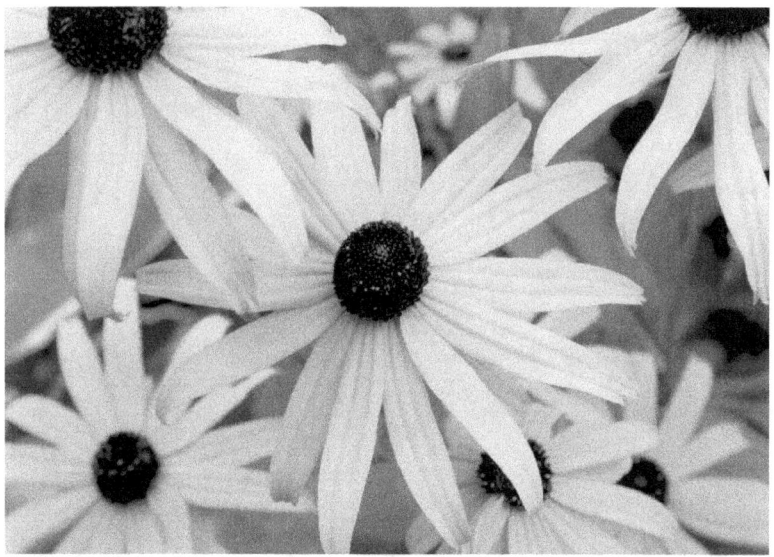

L. L. Smith 2010 Daisies

Also experiment with photo composition by zooming in and turning the camera at different angles to take the photo.

For lake or desert scenes, use a wide angle lens setting. The scene should fill 75% of the frame with a clear blue sky. With cloud formations, it can be a 50/50 scene and sky framing.

When photographing wild animals, insects, and rodents fill the frame and shoot from a safe distance. People are hurt every year from getting too close to animals in national parks.

Macro photography is when you fill the frame with let's say a fly's face or a side view of a frog snapping up a bug with its tongue.

When there several of the same item, such as in the photo of the daisies, composing the image according to the rule of thirds can help.

The idea is to look through the viewfinder and scan the area until something jumps out at you that says, "pick me." Then center the item in the middle of the viewfinder frame, focus and take the photo without fill flash if it is a cloudy day.

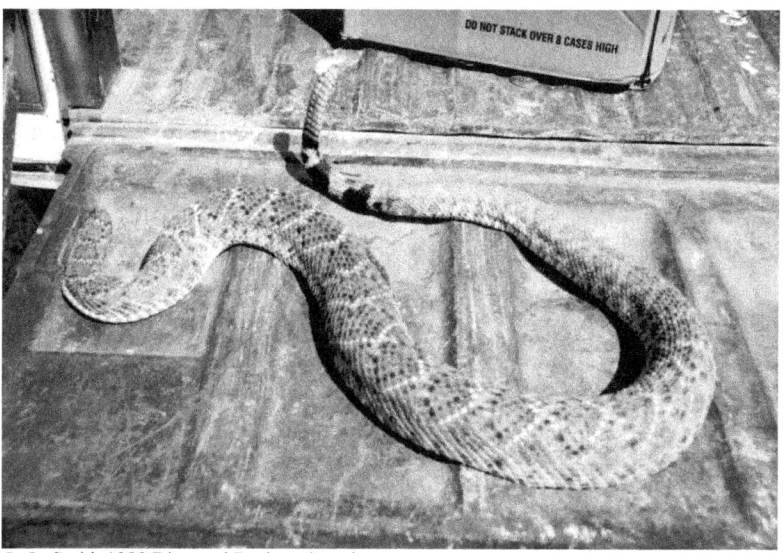

L. L. Smith 1998 Diamond Back rattlesnake

If it is a bright sunny day you will probably have to reposition yourself to avoid a shadow you on the item. Even then, the high overhead sun tends to washout the colors. It is better to shoot in the morning or later in the afternoon.

When taking a photo of a plant in a shaded area outside or inside, instead of using the on camera direct flash, use your external flash set up for diffused lighting. The ASA setting for outdoors is 100 and indoors is 400.

When I lived in Arizona, I use to go out into the desert for recreational activities and saw my fair share of snakes, lizards, scorpions, and spiders.

One time I was out target shooting with a friend when he encountered a six foot rattlesnake that reared up in a striking position. He shot the snake with his Colt 357 through the mouth. He laid the snake on his truck tailgate and snapped a photo. I took the 4" x 6" print into work with me and sold twenty 11" x 14"s for $15.00 each to my male coworkers.

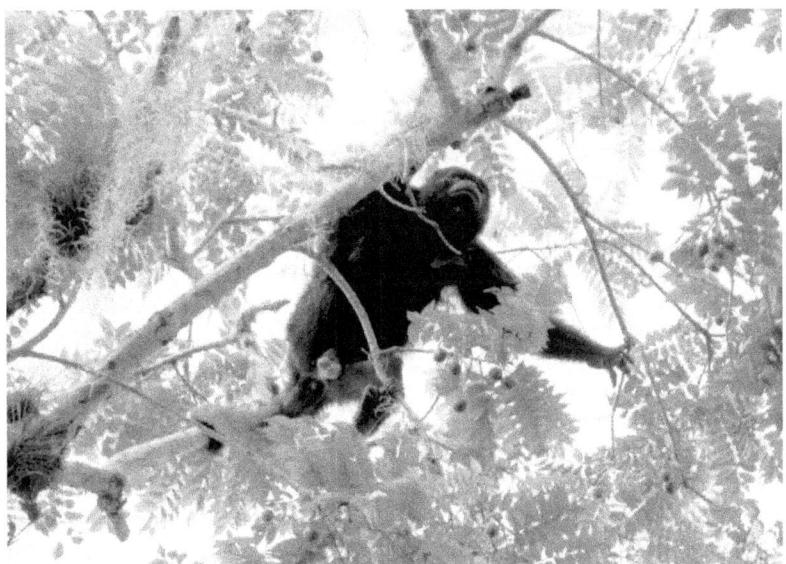

L. L. Smith 2006 Ape in trees, Guatemala

When traveling to a tropic area or jungle, I consider looking up to be a safety factor.

In addition to moving out of the path of falling coconuts from palm trees in Hawaii, I discovered apes like to throw things at people.

On a private guided tour through an archeological dig site in Guatemala that was not open to the public, I felt something hard hit my head. I looked up to see an ape 100 feet above me in the trees, throwing nuts at our group. I used my telephoto lens to get the photo above before moving out of the way.

When photographing a mountain scene--move the mountain to either side of the frame so it slopes gracefully into the scene. The photo below is of the Superstition Mountains in Arizona and was taken in April at 4:00 p.m.

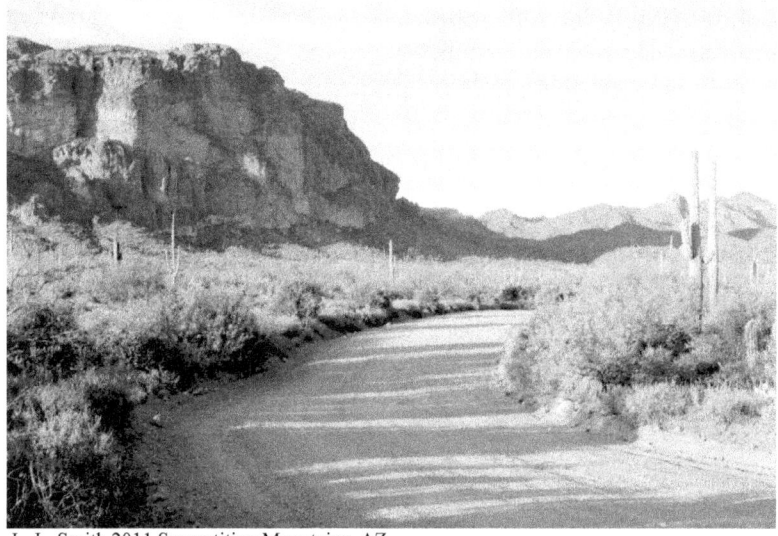

L. L. Smith 2011 Superstition Mountains, AZ

This was the right time to take this winter time desert photo, which created color richness and depth to the scene. The road in the foreground looks as if it is inviting the visitor to keep traveling on to see what's around the next corner.

Some scenery shots, such as the bridge on the next page would have been just so-so if the two people had not been crossing it. And since the people are not identifiable, I don't need a model release to sell this image.

Speaking of model releases, even when traveling in a foreign country, a model release is needed from people with identifiable faces, or privately owned homes or businesses, or sculptures. However, asking for a model release from the locals in a foreign country who don't speak English, will get you a strange look.

When I was visiting a tourist town in Guatemala, a 10 year old street vendor girl dressed in colorful garb, saw me take a photo of her. She then approached me and asked for $5.00 U.S. denomination, which at that time equaled $35.00 in Guatemalan currency. The tour guide had already told me earlier not to give money to kids who begged. This was because parents would have their children beg for money from tourists and then take the money from the kids.

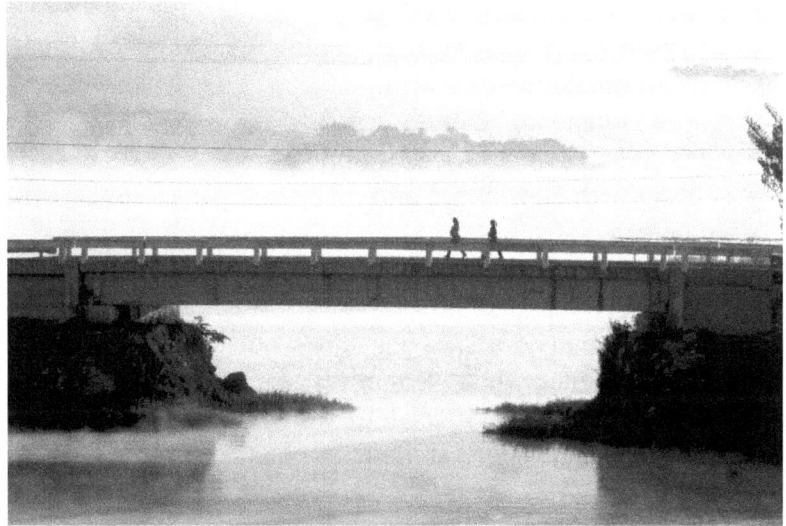

L. L. Smith 2006 People on Bridge, Guatemala

After that I resorted to using my telephoto lens setting and took my photos from a distance or hid where I could not be seen. Because of that, I don't have model releases from the people and the photos cannot be sold.

Chapter 6 THE ART OF SELLING

The art of selling consists not only of marketing but listening and communication skills. The professional photographer needs to be an effective listener in order to confidently communicate with people. This is done by:

- Maintaining a positive and happy attitude while
- Listening to and answering people's questions accurately and in a timely manner with…
- Proper English and diction in a
- Pleasant and even toned voice plus
- Smiling with confidence and maintaining eye contact with the person.

6.1 The Essence of Listening

Effective listening is a skill that does not come naturally to most people. Hence when we don't listen effectively, it causes misunderstandings which lead to disagreements and fights. Therefore, good listening skills take practice in order to gain empathy, respect, and trust from our clients.

Over the span of our life time we learn and use many rude and inconsiderate bad listening habits and behaviors such as:

- Interrupting a conversation with our point of view

- Rolling our eyes in disgust or disagreement

- Raising our eyebrows in disapproval

- Yawning, sighing, or deep breaths and exhaling with moans

- Looking away and curling our lips

- Glaring at a person and shaking our head

- Sitting with our arms crossed when someone we don't like or care for is talking

- Allowing distractions to interrupt conversations

- Not turning off our cell phones or other media when someone is speaking

- Pretending to listen but not hearing what is being said

So to break those bad habits we need to understand there are three levels of listening. The first level is basically where people are more interested in talking than listening. You see this when two people are talking at the same time and no one is listening.

Level two is where a person pretends to hear what someone is saying... but is distracted instead of making the effort to comprehend what the speaker means.

For example like when a couple is dining together at a restaurant and the woman is talking about an important matter that needs resolving. The man will nod his head and say "yes dear" as if he is listening, while sending a text on his cell phone. Then when the woman asks for the man's input on the matter, he looks up and says "What did you say dear?"

Level three is called 'active listening' where a person is using their ears *to listen* so they *can hear* what is being said in order *to processes* the speaker's message so they can *understand* what it means. This is when you are paying attention to what a person is saying and comprehend it at the same time.

Another advantage of being an active listener is when difficult people try to engage you in an argument. Because when you activity listen instead of engaging, an argument can't start. When they realize their tactics aren't working, they give up and move on to a weaker target to engage.

So just how do you master the active listening stage? Here is the cut-to-the-chase version:

Using direct eye contact with the speaker

Americans use direct eye contact when speaking, but Asians and Native American Indians will turn their eyes away or look down. However, they are still listening to what you are saying? So keep on talking and then ask for verification of what you said when finished.

Also do not get distracted by the conversations and activities around you and turn away to see what's going on. Keep your eye contact focused on the speaker.

Using positive body language
When at a table you should sit up straight and rest your hands on the table joined together in a relax hold. Or set your hands in your lap. Don't prop your arm up on the table and rest your head in an open palm while tapping a pen or pencil. And don't cross your arms.

Acknowledging with validation
Nod your head every so often to indicate you understand what the speaker is saying. When you are speaking to Asian people, they smile a lot but it does not mean they understand what you say. To avoid misunderstanding you need to validate with statements such as:

"Mr. Chang, so I understand, you want me to make sure your mother is to be in the center of the front row in all the family photos, correct?"

The same principle of validation applies to all conversations.

Be clear with clarification
If you don't understand what the client wants, don't feel shy or embarrassed to ask questions to clarify what was said. This avoids misunderstands that can lead to future arguments or disagreements at a job.

Leave the ego out of the conversation
When you meet with any client, it is not your place to judge them, or give your personal opinion about their personal belief system or lifestyle. You are there to listen, maintain eye contact, smile, nod your head, and validate. If you don't like and disapprove of the client or they irritate you, then do not do the job. It will only lead to problems.

To further help develop good communication and listening skills, there are organizations such as **Toastmasters** that give members ample opportunities on public speaking.

6.2 Time to Answer the Phone

Here is a sentence from a phone answering service ad I found interesting: *"A recent study found that between 30 and 50% of people who call a business don't leave a message if they get voice mail or an answering machine. Instead they hang up."*

The obvious goal of the ad was to convey that a business needed to answer their phone at all times, or risk losing customers. But what if you can't answer your phone at all times. Should you use an answering service?

A Google search using the words answering services showed over 16 million results. The top ten company results had pricing as low as $9.99 a month up to $39.99 a month.

But you don't need to resort to an answering service because if you have the right kind of voice message, people will leave a message.

When people call your business and they get your voice mail or answering machine, your voice needs to sound professional and pleasant.

This means no boring and casual tone of voice, or like you just woke up, or speaking in a hurried tone of voice that makes the person's call sound like it is an imposition.

And don't let your kids answer the phone or leave the voice message. Your child is special to you and immediate family.

However, they are not special to the customer and therefore the customer will hang up .

In the early 1990's I had a boyfriend who allowed his nine year old daughter to record the voice message on my business phone. At the time I was getting three to four calls a day, but then one day they stopped. When I checked the caller ID, I would see new numbers but no voice messages had been left.

Three days later my sister called me and asked "Whose kid is on your phone message?" I said I had no idea and ended the call to investigate. I called my business phone, and when I heard the boyfriend's daughter's voice, I was livid. I immediately recorded a new voice greeting.

When I told the boyfriend not to do that again, he became upset and thought I was being over reactive. Needless to say that relationship did not last.

A voice message should be short and to the point instead of a long message. The following is an effective and short voice message script template that you can use:

"Hello. You have reached (Your company name). I am not able to take your call at this time—but please leave your name… a number you can be reached at… and a message… and I will call you back as soon as possible. Thank you for calling and have a great day."

Practice reading a phone script until it sounds unrushed, smooth and with a smile and lightness to your voice.

Have someone listen to you read the script and give you their feedback and critique.

To avoid coughing from a dry throat, take a drink of water before recording the message. If you have a raspy voice, have someone else record the message for you. Large company's do it all the time.

When you get a call, check the caller ID to see who's calling. That way you can switch to your business greeting voice.

6.3 Questions to ask Your Client

In order to be prepared to do the job right, ask questions. The following is a list of questions to ask a client:

- *Is flash allowed in the church?* You will need a tripod for non flash photos in a church—so always keep one in your car as it is easy to forget to take it when you leave the house. This avoids the embarrassment asking if someone at the wedding has one you can borrow.

- *Where is the event being held?* It is good to research and become familiar with the venue.

- *What is the number of couples I will be photographing?* If this is for a company party—you can give your pricing quote from your fee schedule over the phone.

- *How many people are in the wedding party?* If there are 20 couples all wanting photos with the bridal couple, you'll probably go over the 35 minute formal photo time limit.

- *Do you want photographs before the wedding?* For a backyard wedding, photographing the bridal party and family before hand is recommended. Because when the ceremony is over the guests and family will approach bridal couple with well wishes and endless questions. When I was hired for my two hour plan—I also staged and photographed the cake cutting, toast and signing the marriage license.

- *Is there a wedding coordinator?* Most wedding coordinators are professional and polite. However, there are the difficult ones that have unreasonable rules that may hinder you from performing your job. In that case let the bride know. She will probably tell the coordinator—"forget the rules—my photographer is going to do what they have to do to get my photos".

- *Are you going to another location to do the formal photos?* Decide how far you will travel to a second location before implementing a travel charge. Myself, I did not charge extra for secondary locations.

- *If parents are remarried*—ask how well they all get along with each other.

- *Are there any small children in the wedding?* Use gum and candy mints as a reward/enticement for the kids to be good and smile during formal photos.

Questions from the Client

Here are questions you may be asked during the interview:

- *How long have you been photographing weddings?*

- *Do I receive all my prints in an album?*

- *Do you put your studio name on the proofs?*

- *Do you have copyright marks on the photos?*

- *Do you have a list of the photos you take during the wedding and reception? Here is the list:*
  - The bridal couple getting ready and other pre-wedding activities
  - The groomsmen lighting the candles in the candelabras
  - The grandmothers and mothers being seated
  - The mothers lighting candles on the side of the unity candle
  - The wedding party processional
  - All events during the ceremony—rings exchange, unity candle, readings, people singing
  - The recessional of bridal party and the parents
  - Formal photos of the family, wedding party, bridal couple and the rings
  - Bridal party out by the limo
  - The bridal party, parents and grandparents entrance into the reception hall
  - Table photos of guests, cake, gift table, and table decorations
  - Any other photo requests from family and guests
  - The toasts, cake cutting, and garter and bouquet toss
  - The bridal and groom going through the buffet line
  - The first dance, family and wedding party dances, and guests dancing

- Any candid moments or events that occur during the reception

Can my family and guests take photos too or do you insist upon exclusive rights? Be a good sport, let family members take photos with their cell phones and P & S cameras.

How do you dress for the job? Even though I dressed professionally for an interview—I still would have to explain what I was going to wear.

Do you have an assistant? I didn't have an assistant. Another business no-no I encountered as a bridesmaid in my friend's wedding, was when the photographer brought along a student and was teaching her as he took the formal photographs. We were at the church 1.5 hours.

Do you charge extra for touch ups? When I shot film, I charged extra because people would assume they were included. When digital came along, I removed it from the agreement form and told the client that editing was the touching up process.

How long do you keep the original negatives in case we want to order an album later on? I told the couple I stored the photos on DVD's and had a five year time limit before discarding—not destroying—the images.

Do you offer Ala Carte pricing on albums? I offered ala carte pricing on albums, coffee table books, DVD slide shows, enlargements, and other products.

Do you have online ordering so our families can order from you? A necessity in today's digital world.

Do you do special photo requests? People would give me a list of requests that were similar to the list of the photos I took.

How long will it take you to do the formal photos after the wedding? I had my time down to 35 minutes because I kept it moving. Move about that later on.

What is your turn around time on getting the photos to us? The turnaround time is one of those unique selling points (USP) that will set you apart from the competition. Instead of making couples wait a month or longer for their finished product you can say with a smile, "Your album will be ready by the time you return from your honeymoon." The client will love you for it.

What is your deposit? How do you take payment? Can I pay everything up front? Always get a deposit of at least a third of the plan price. Or set an amount that will cover your expenses plus some profit. Mine was $250.00.

It is usually not a wise thing to take the entire payment upfront, especially if the wedding is six or more months away. Instead have a payment schedule where the entire amount is paid a week before the wedding.

Stipulate the time limit after the deposit will not be refundable. My non-refundable time period was one week. Also, people prefer paying with debit and credit cards, hence you should have a credit card merchant account, or one of those credit card cubes from **Squareup.com** that fits onto the I Phone. There is a small fee for each transaction.

If you decide to accept full payment the day of the wedding, and the client says, "oh, I don't have my checkbook with me, can I pay you when I get back from the honeymoon?"—take out your I-Phone and credit card cube, smile, and say, "No problem, I do accept credit or debit."

Do you have back up equipment? A no brainer and already discussed.

How many locations will you travel to and do you have a travel fee? If the location was further than 60 miles round trip I had a $20 travel fee.

Do fussy and crying children bother you? *Gum and Mintos worked miracles.*

Do you have liability insurance? Having insurance is a personal decision. I explained to people that a lawyer friend of mine said that since I did not have a storefront, I did not need insurance. However I had this clause in my agreement form:

'Photography by Laura is not held responsible for and from any injuries and or damages due to children and/or guests running into or tripping over photographer's equipment. If the photographer equipment is damaged by the clients, guests, or their children, they shall be responsible for replacing the equipment with the same product or cash equivalent'.

Do you have an overtime fees? This is not advisable. Please refer to Keeping Up Your Profit Base on page 135.

Do you give discounts for Sundays, holidays, and military families? I never understood why studios and photographers gave a Sunday discount. Think about it, you will work just as hard on a Sunday as you will on a Saturday or a holiday. So hence I had no discount. The military discount is up to your discretion.

Do you have several portfolio books I can look at? You should have a proof album, two enlargement albums of 8" x 10"s, a 5" x 7" album, and a photo book.

Do you have a refund policy? I was leery of brides-to-be who asked too many questions about refunds.

I had this one bridal couple that when they came to get their photos, sat for 45 minutes looking at their album. They liked what they saw, paid me, and left. A week later the bride called asking for a $150.00 refund because she did not like certain photos. I said "I'm sorry to hear that but according to the agreement form you signed, once the client looks at, pays and takes possession of the photos and leaves there is no refunds."

"Well (husband's name) and I are not happy with the way some of the photos are," and then she went into detail about what they did not like. I listened and when she was finished I said…

"I'm sorry you feel that way, but you and (husband' name) sat for 45 minute looking at the photos and never pointed out any of what you have told me. A matter of fact you both said the photos were great and you were happy with them".

"Well, I only said that because you made (husband's name) and me feel rushed so we really did not have the time to examine the photos closer. And since that time we are finding things wrong in the pictures that we don't like and we think you should refund us back the $150.00".

I then repeated, "I'm sorry you feel that way, but according to the agreement form you signed, you examined the photos, paid, and took the photos home. So I am sorry that I cannot give you a refund."

The bride then said, "You know you are so unprofessional. You ruined an otherwise beautiful day by giving me horrible photos, and then you won't even refund me what I think is a fair amount. It's obvious I'm not getting anywhere with you. And don't even think about getting referrals from me!" And she hung up. I wasn't bothered by the call because I knew she was suffering from buyers' remorse.

6.4 Clinching the Deal

I had a medium sized rolling suitcase that I used to carry my business cards, price lists, brochures, wedding agreement forms, and wedding portfolio books.

When meeting with clients, arrive at least 15 minutes early. Set out the portfolio books in front of the client's seat. Then assemble a business card, the pricing, and photo sheet to hand the client after the introductions and they are seated.

If people do not show up at the scheduled time, call them after about 15 minutes. If you get their voice mail leave a message such as "Hello, I am here at the location and waiting for you.

Please call me back as soon as you can as I will be leaving in 15 minutes. Thank you."

After giving your sales presentation, when the couple is sitting across from you thinking and discussing what they have seen, *say nothing.*

Also do not disturb the couples thought process by blurting out something like "Oh I'll give you an additional 10% if you book with me today."

By doing this you have broken the golden rule of sales ***If the photographer speaks first they lose.***

Always let the client's speak first because they will usually say, "We have decided we're going to hire you."

If the couple says instead that they *"want to think about it"*, and your reply is, "Okay, nice to have met you," and you let them leave without you obtaining a commitment, this is the death of the sale. The following is an example of what to say:

Client: "We are going to think about it and will let you know."

You: "All right sounds good. As a convenience I am going to give you a copy of my agreement form. That way if you decide to hire me, you will have it handy to fill out and sent back to me."

And as you hand it to the clients say, "So when do you think you will be making a decision?" This requires the client to committing to something. Once you have their reply you say:

"Okay, sounds good. So I will do a follow up call on that day. Do you have a preferred time that you would like me to call?"

Again the prospective client is committed to giving you a time to call. Then you validate that by saying:

"Okay (client's name) sounds good I will be calling on (date) at (time). It has been a pleasure meeting with you both and I look forward to talking with you again. You two have a good rest of the day".

If the client does not call back at the time they said, you call them. If the client does not give you a time or date, call them back by the third business day. Because, follow-up calls are not being pushy or aggressive. And if the people do not hire you, ask why by saying:

"Okay, (person's name) may I have your feedback on why you did not hire me so it can help me improve on what I can offer my clients?" Then thank the person for their answer.

6.5 You've Got Objections

I have on my wall the phrase that motivational speaker and author Zig Ziglar once said, *"Every sale has five basic obstacles: need, money, hurry, desire, and trust."* [13] So to overcome objections—the key is to know how to respond.

- *We found someone who is only charging $400.00 for the same package you are offering. Are you willing to match the other guy's price?*
  I have heard this bluff quite a few times and would say, "I'm sorry, but I am going to have to pass. Sounds like you should go with the other guy."

  Either the people may try to renegotiate with a "Well we really like your work and would like to hire you but" or they will say good-bye and hang up.

  Regardless the bottom line is—don't lower your price.

- *A family member/friend is photographing the wedding.*
  Give the person a business card and say, "Here's my card in case something happens where the family member/friend can't be there or decides not to be the photographer. And by the way, I went to a friend's wedding where they had her uncle as the photographer and he left the rolls of film in a hot car and the negatives were ruined. Luckily, I had brought

my camera and took pictures. She was so glad that she paid me.

- *We want our photographer to be insured.*
There is photography insurance coverage available in case the photos don't come out or are lost due to computer malfunction and you are taken to court.

- *You're not professional enough.*
You will probably hear this because of your working out of your home instead of having a store front or you have no four year degree. You might want to point out because you do work out of your home that is how you can offer affordable priced services. And that you accept credit cards and are a member of a business association such as the local **chamber of commerce** or a **business networking group**.

- *We're going with another company because they offer something you don't have.*
If it is something that you have access to and can provide, offer it to the client.

6.6 Surveys & Referrals—The Key to More Work

When meeting with the client to give them their photos—the four words to get referrals is—"I need your help." People are more than happy to help you and will give you at least one name. Here is a script you can say with those four words.

"John and Mary, *I need your help*. Since I know you are happy and satisfied with my service and love the photos, (give a smile) do you mind giving me the names of three people you think would enjoy having the same positive experience?"

A week after the client has their photos, you should use the postal service instead of email to mail a thank you card, along with a survey and provide a SASE. The survey should be short and easy to fill out.

The following is the survey template I mailed to clients. It had a section at the bottom for the client to write comments. When

I posted the comments on my website, I used only the person's first name and last initial.

Dear (Client name)

I am always striving to make my services better for my client's. Can you take a few moments of your time and fill out the survey and mail it back in the SASE? You help is very much appreciated. Your personal information will remain confidential. Thank you.

                                   Very Satisfied   Satisfied   Unsatisfied
1.Print quality of the photographs
2.Activities photographed in a timely manner?
3.Promptness of photographer
4.Photographer's courteousness
5.Flexibility in accommodating requests
6.Photography package pricing
7.How was your overall experience with my service?
Would you consider me for your future photography needs? Yes No
Would you recommendation me to others? Yes   No

Please add any other comments or suggestions
_____
_____
_____

Date of wedding: _____
Name: _____
Address: _____
City: _____ Zip: _____
Phone (   ) _____ Email: _____

Photography by Your Company
Creating Smiles one Photo at a Time
Web site: yourcompany@abc.com
Your email Phone: 555-555-5555

I also mailed clients anniversary and Christmas cards. I ordered calendars from The National Pen Company, **www.pens.com** and mailed them to clients.

Another way to develop a business relationship and get referrals is to exchange cards and website links with the DJ's, florists, cake people, limo companies, and caterers you meet at weddings and other events.

Chapter 7 BRINGING IN THE BUSINESS

As a photographer I had an 80/20 rule that I ascribed to, 80% of my business was marketing and advertising to bring in the customers and 20% was using my technical knowledge to shoot the pictures. Because, unless I had paying customers, my technical skills were just idling.

Marketing your business is all about your client population, it is not about you. This means knowing what client's want, having a web site that targets the right client, proof books with photos that are client centered , using client feedback to improve, and pricing that is geared for everyone, just not the high end client.

It is also about putting a 110% effort into all aspects of your business. Plus, having and exhibiting a positive and upbeat attitude that shows you enjoy what you're doing.

Marketing also means, NO EXCUSES. The client does not care or wants to hear why you were late and missed taking the wedding ceremony processional, or why you did not get that important candid shot, or how you lost the photos because your CF died, or whatever. Excuses are the death of your reputation, will not get you future referrals, and can be financially costly if the photo job is ruined.

This chapter focuses on building a photography business platform. Topics covered are:

- Welcoming clients to your home

- Building your portfolio albums

- The right SEO and copywriting that gets attention

- Using free advertising to attract clientele

- Communication techniques: knowing when to listen and talk

- Marketing materials such as brochures, pricing sheets, agreement forms, business cards, calendars and more

- Using social media such as blogs, LinkedIn, Twitter, Facebook, and Word Press to promote you

7.1 Locating the Happy Bridal Couple

After twenty years of photographing weddings here is what I learned about bridal couples.

The couple, especially the bride, expects everyone to be as excited and happy as they are. They think that their wedding is more unique and important than any other couple you have ever photographed before, and think they are more special. The couple will settle for nothing less than perfection, will not tolerate excuses, and will expect you to bend over backwards to accommodate every special request.

This why you schmooze the bridal couple to make them feel like they are the only client you have.

And, even though you will see the same bridal dress styles, cakes, table decorations, and candid photo moments again and again—you still need to tell the bride how beautiful, unique, creative, and great everything looks.

Plus when you should always point out how much fun you had photographing their wedding, how nice everyone was, how cute the kids were, and how they were so easy to work with. And let the bride hug you as she leaves. Because, that is how you get referred to her friends for more business.

7.2 Welcoming Clients to Your Home

As a home-based photographer, you will be faced with two options on where you can photograph and meet clients:

1. If you have small children, a messy home, or you don't have the room, you will have to go to peoples home. This option places limits on doing photo work in your home.

2. If you have the room, clients will be able come to your home to conduct business and or have photos taken. For this option, you will need an area of your home that is not part of

the living area that the family or pets use. The area should be:

- Roomy enough to put up your studio lighting and backdrops

- Have a draped off changing area or a clean bathroom

- A place to showcase your high quality albums, and products such as photo pillows, blankets, cups, plus your framed enlargements of your work and awards on the walls

- Have a place where clients can sit to watch a DVD slide show and

- Before your client arrives, have your portfolios and marketing materials set up and ready in your viewing area. Plus turn on music to play quietly and softly in the background

After you have lead the client's to your home studio/office area, always offer them a beverage such as water, coffee, tea, or a soft drink.

7.3 Creating your Portfolio Albums

The hardcopy portfolio albums that showcase your work are assembled with professional wedding albums. These albums are purchased through a professional album dealer in your area. The generic photo albums that are sold in the big box discount and craft stores are not recommended.

The top four professional album manufactures are:

Renaissance Albums—this website has a digital catalogue and you can buy directly from the site. They sell flush mount enlargement albums.

Topflight albums—this site offers specials and also sells the **TAP** proof book and enlargement albums.

Art Leather Albums—these are only available through professional photo album dealers.

Wedding album depot and **Wedding albums and more—** sites that offer all brands of professional albums.

Tyndell Photographic Packaging is located in Livonia, MI. They sell both a white or black 4" x 6" Thrifty Choice Album that is made in the U.S.A. The white album is embossed with a flower design and the words 'Our Wedding' on the front. The albums are priced under $30.00 at the time of this writing.

These are the proof albums referred to in this guide. They can also be used for a portfolio book. Each proof book comes in a black cardboard box with both clear photo inserts and white order sheets. Each clear photo inserts holds six photos.[14]

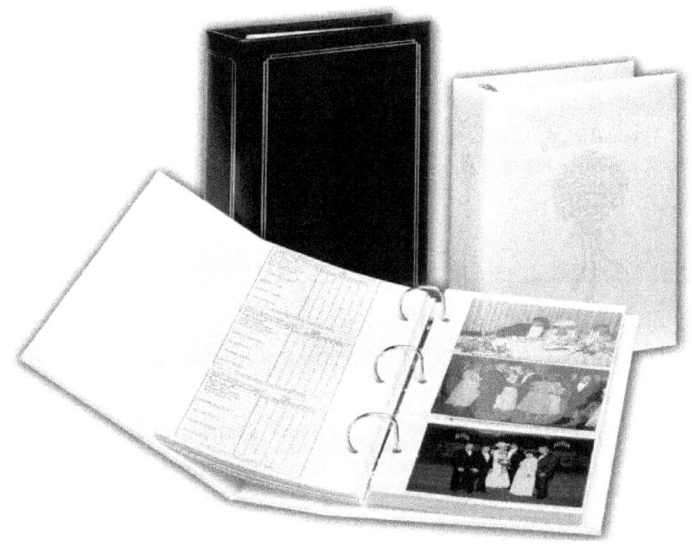

Tyndell Photo 2014

Creating Your Portfolio

This is what your portfolio album collection should consist of:

- One 4" x 6" proof book with 300 assorted wedding photos

- One Renaissance 5" x 7" flush mount album with 24 photos

- One Renaissance 8" x 10" flush mount with 24 photos

- One TAP album with photo inserts with 24—8" x 10's and 48—5" x 7"s

- One custom 8" x 10" hardcover photo book and one 5" x 7" paperback photo book. I used **My Publisher**, but they are going out of business. I also have used **Shutterfly**, and I liked the quality of the photo books.

7.4 The Selling Power of a Web Site

Savvy business owners know that a professionally developed web site that focuses on what the client's wants, is what brings in the business.

Case in point, my eleven page photography website had visitors calling me and saying, "I love your website, you have so many different photos showing all the wedding and reception, just not a few, I want to hire you. Are you available for this date and where do I mail the deposit?"

Now I know you would love to hear that too, and you can with the right website and domain name. To develop a domain name, it is a good idea to write out different name ideas to find what fits your business.

When you have the one you feel is right, **Godaddy.com** sells and registers domain names for a nominal fee. You type in your business name the search box and the info pops up letting you know if it already exists. If it does, then you tweak it till you find the right one.

There are hundreds of website building resources on the Internet? It is mind boggling, so to save you time searching here are 13 of the better ones out on the web.

WordPress.com—is one of the easiest and quickest ways to get up a web site. A premium site only costs $99.00 a year and you can use your domain, set up the pages you want upload photos, and create a side bar with widgets. There are videos and tutorials that will help you set up your web site. I have my **Clicking for Cash from Home** blog at this site complete with photos.

Bludomain.com—starts at $50.00

clickbooq.com –Offers a 14 day free trial

intothedarkroom.com –Photography websites, blogs, photo carts, slideshows, hosting and more.

Here are a few more:

- **jalbum.net**
- **Jimdo.com**
- **photobiz.com**
- **portfoliositez.com**

- **Squarespace.com**
- **smugmug.com**
- **stunningwebsites**
- **weebly.com**

You can also hire a professionally trained web developer to build your nine page web site. Avoid having a family member, friend, or the college kid who claim to know computers, but has no graphic design knowledge. Plus you should retain the ability to log on to your website to add photographs and make changes to the copy.

I avoided the type of website that featured a slideshow of only my best 50 wedding photos with romantic music playing, an ego based 'about us' page with my philosophy of life, a long bio with over-kill on education and awards, and a 'contact us' page to get my pricing. Because I know that…

People are busy and when they visit a site, they want information. They don't care and won't read about my philosophy of life, education, awards, and a long bio. And unless visitors are professional photographers themselves, they won't know what CMPP or other exclusive professional photography titles are or even mean. Plus…

Visitors to a site want simplicity. If a websites 'contact us' page form is too long, instead of just name, email and phone number, the visitor will move on to the competition.

You should also avoid using the Google Adsense program that places ads on your website landing or home page. Pop-up ads are another business killer because they cover what your visitor is reading. The same goes for pop-unders which automatically displays in a second smaller browser window upon opening a web page.

So to keep your visitors focused on what you have to offer… Here are the eleven pages to include on the website side bar the visitor can click on to read and learn more.

HOME

This is also known as your website landing page. It should have a banner with your company name and tagline i.e. (your company) Creating Smiles one Photo at a Time. It should also have a short blurb and link to key pages such as the wedding and portrait photography, services, albums, and products.

ABOUT THE COMPANY

This page should open with your mission statement:
- At (your company) we believe in providing our clients with quality service and products at reasonable and affordable pricing. We go the extra mile by taking the time to do the job right and to ensure your satisfaction. We believe in the old fashion way of being honest and ethical to gain your trust and business. We look forward to talking with you to show you want we can do for you.

Also include a professional business photo, tag line, a *short* bio of educational background, charitable work and a thank you tip for visiting the website: (use this one or create one)

- As a thank-you for visiting our site (Company name) would like to share with you a "professional" photo taking technique. You can use this tip at home to create your own professional style outdoor portraits any time and any where…

Then explain something like the steps of the outdoor fill light technique of using a light color wall on page 51.

PHOTOGRAPHY SERVICES

At the top of my services page, I had a 1.5 minute example of my $125.00 DVD slide show that was created with Pinnacle Studios. Then I listed a description of services and what I included as part of the packages. Here are the different photography services I offered:

- Weddings
- Special lifestyle weddings
- Engagement sessions
- Bar-bat mitzvahs
- Quinceaneras
- Anniversary & Birthday Parties
- Wedding & Baby Showers
- Corporate & Special Events
- In home family & on location portraits
- Pets, Products & Artwork
- Creating wedding albums
- DVD slide shows
- Photo restoration & editing

PRICING & PRODUCTS

This page describes the plans and pricing. The following wedding plan and pricing copy is an example:

All the wedding plans include the 4" x 6" prints in a beautiful and embossed proof album. A CD with all the edited images, plus your choice of enlargements.

Ultimate Plan $2500.00—Includes 7 to 9 hours. A photo CD of engagement photo session. 300—4" x 6" prints in album & CD. An enlargement album of 12-8" x 10"s & 24-5" x 7"s or flush mount album of 10 pages, 20 sides. A 16" x 20" framed photograph and coffee table book.

Premier Plan $1275.00—9 hours: Over 300-4"x6" prints in album, 10-8"x10"s, 8-5"x7"s, & photo CD.

Deluxe Plan $1075.00—6 hours: Up to 300-4"x6" prints in album, 8-8"x10"s, 6-5"x7"s, & photo CD

Standard Plan $825.00—4 hours: Up to 275-4"x6" prints in album, 4-8"x10"s, 6-5"x7"s, & photo CD.

- Engagement session............................. $125.00

- Photo light & back drop..............................$ 50.00
- Enlargement Album. 12-8" x 10"s & 24-5" x 7"....$675.00
- Art Leather Flush mount album-10 pgs, 20 sides $675.00
- Parents Album. 24-5" x 7"s........................ $299.00
- Framed 16" x 20" framed enlargement............. $135.00
- Photo Blanket 54" x 70"-Your photo choice... $125.00
- Photo pillow- (Your choice of photo)............... $ 39.99
- DVD Event Album.................................. $125.00
- Hard cover coffee table book (15 pgs/30 sides).. $135.00
- Digital brag books (15 pgs/ 30 sides)............... $ 39.99

Reprint and Enlargement pricing:

- 4" x 6"........$2.25
- 5" x 7"........$5.50
- 8" x 10".......$12.50
- 11" x 14".......$25.00
- 16" x 20".......$45.50
- 20" x 30".......$65.00

WEDDING GALLERY

It is acceptable to post photos from your photo jobs on your web site or use them for your own promotional purposes. It is unacceptable, and can get you sued—to sell or rent the images to anyone, unless you obtain permission or a model release from the client.

Before adding photos to your wedding gallery the file size and picture dimensions need to be reduced. This can be done using Microsoft Office Picture Manager.

- Select the pictures you want to compress, copy the originals, and move them into a new folder.

- Next click on the first photo in the folder and open it with the Microsoft Office Picture Manager. When the Picture manager opens, click on the picture tab at the top and chose compress pictures.

- A box will open on the right side of the screen. Click on Web pages, and then click okay. Click under file to save.

- All pictures will be saved to a compressed file format and resized to fit within a window or 448 x 336 pixels.

The two unique selling points (USP) of my website were, the affordable pricing and wedding gallery photo page.

Useful Tip: *When starting out, set yourself apart from the high priced guys and offer a great product at a reasonable price. When you get a reputation of being good, trustworthy, and dependable, and get more work than you can handle, that is the time to raise your prices.*

A diverse wedding gallery should have at least 225 photos showing every aspect of a wedding. All photos should be well lit and composed, express emotion, spontaneity, and creativity.

Plus the photos should include close ups, wide angle, tilted, black and white, colorized, and photo painted images.

Because of the diversity of photos in my wedding gallery, when visitors called my phone they commented, "I like it that you have so many different types of wedding photos on your website. All the other websites I have been looking at don't even have half the amount of photos you do, and that is why I want to hire you." This will have you singing, 'ka-ching, more money in the bank!

Please visit the ***Clicking for Cash from Home Word Press*** site to see examples of wedding photos.

Below is a suggested chronological list of photo events during a wedding day. Create a folder and place the photos you want to post. Be sure to balance out the topics. For example—there is no need to post three family group photos. Two will get the point across. On the other hand—you want to make sure you show the bridal couple in every aspect of the wedding day.

- The bride and groom arriving and getting ready

- The bride coming down the aisle during the processional

- Ring exchange, unity candle lighting,

- Wide angle photos from back of church and from balconies

- Bridal couples coming down the aisle during the processional

- Bridal couple photos

- Rings on hands over bridal bouquet

- Bridal party doing fun and spontaneous things with the bride and groom and by the limo

- Bridal couple outside in front of church and other venues

- Bridal couple entering reception

- Toasts, cake cutting, bridal couple dance, father daughter, mother son, wedding party, and guests dancing

- The garter and bouquet toss

- Candid and cute kid, sentimental family, and fun guest moments that occur during the ceremony and reception.

- Table photos of guests, food, cakes, gift tables, and table decorations

When you take photos of table decorations or center pieces, don't forget to move aside the water pitchers, glasses, salt and pepper shakers, butter dishes and other items.

Photos of table decorations, flowers, shoes, the backs of dresses, bow ties, glassware and other items is what I refer to as product shots. These shots should not be more 15% of your wedding gallery.

After all you're photographing a wedding, not an advertising layout for a company or manufacturer.

Now if you want to take extra wedding product shots at a photo job and sell them as stock images, go for it. Just make sure you shoot those photos in the RAW format, that way you can edit the image according to a premium stock photography sites submission guidelines.

The one style of photograph you might want to sparingly use on your website is where a bridal couple is engulfed by a landscape and you can barely see them. I call this *"people lost in the scenery shot"* syndrome.

I would take the *"people lost in the scenery shot"* if a bridal couple told me specifically they wanted most of the photo to be scenery. Most of those were usually done in front of a church. Otherwise the hand colored photo featured below was the way I photographed my scenery shots.

When I subscribed to the PPA magazine the *"people lost in the scenery shot"* seemed to win the competitions. The bridal couple would be so tiny in the outdoor scene that I couldn't determine if the photographer was shooting for a nature magazine or a wedding.

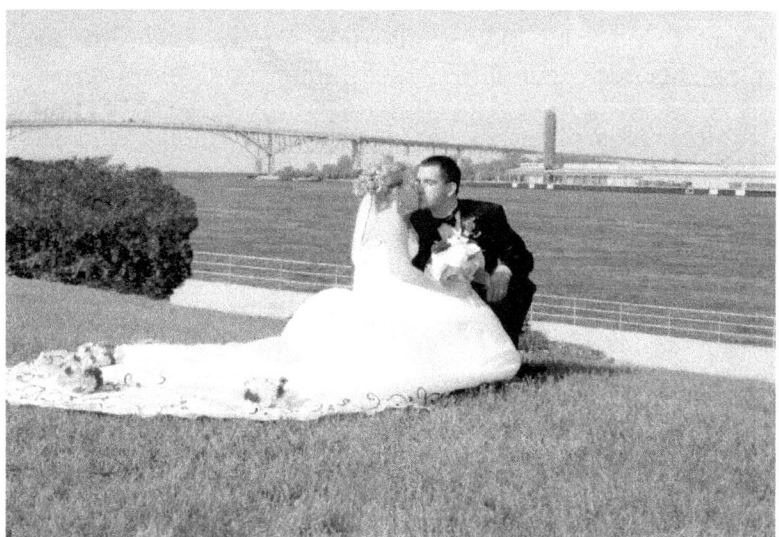

L. L. Smith 2009   Couple by Lake

PORTRAIT GALLERY

At the top of the page you should describe what you include in your photo plans and then list your plans and pricing.

The lower part of the page should show high school seniors and family portraits, business functions, birthdays, baby and wedding showers, pets, home, business, quinceaneras and other ethic events, and other types of photo jobs.

ART GALLERY

This is an optional page to showcase your artistic endeavors such as photo artwork, greeting cards, or books related to photography.

ALBUMS & GIFTS

This page should feature photos and descriptions of albums, photo books, blankets, pillows, photo mugs, and other items. The album photo collage below was created with the **Gary Fong** album software. This software is downloaded into Photoshop 6 or higher.

The Gary Fong program works by opening Photoshop Bridge and choosing the photos you want to drop and drag into the flush mount album design page. When done with designing the album it is saved as a JPEG for printing the photo layout.

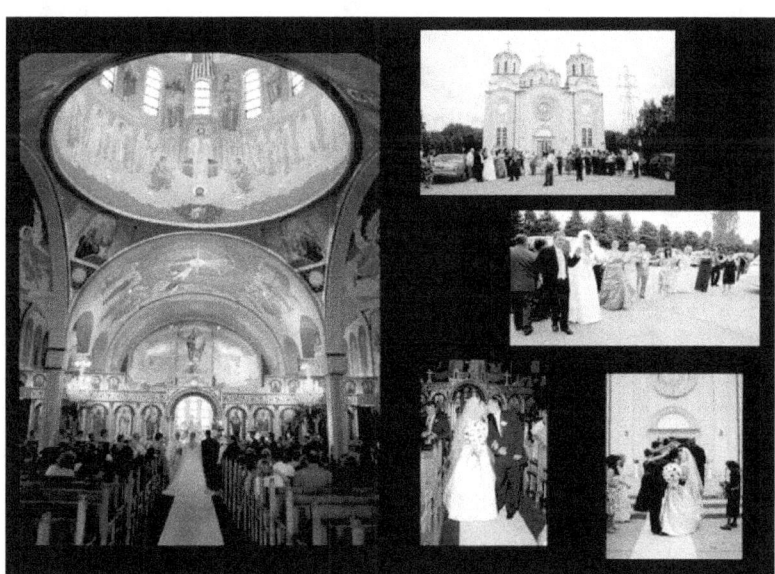

L. L. Smith 2009 Photo collage layout

A flush mount album has pages covered with a protective covering you peel off to expose the adhesive backing. Then a photograph is rolled onto the adhesive carefully. Once the photo is on the page, it is permanent and cannot be removed without being ripped.

Additionally, I found the collage style photographs to be a great sales tool for selling 8" x 10" or 11" x 14" enlargements.

THE LINKS PAGE

This is where you place links to the businesses that reciprocate your business, in other words the ones that refer business to you and vice versa. This page should be where to place the Google Ad Sense ads if you choose to go that route.

TESTIMONIALS—IT'S NOT A CHEESY ACT

When clients are satisfied and happy with your work they will give you their testimonials. When posting don't give the clients entire name, just the first name and last initial. Here are a few examples of testimonials from past clients:

"I want to thank you for the excellent and outstanding job that you did. It was a delight to have you at our wedding. It took us so long to find someone who could do both color and black and white photography-and we really didn't know what to expect since it was so dark that night. I was truly impressed with how wonderfully the photographs came out. It is so terrific to have the entire wedding on film and not to have to choose only 20 pictures or so. **And I was amazed at the fact that every single picture came out!** Everyone who has seen the photos has commented on how great they are and even said that they thought they are so much better than their own wedding pictures. I wish you the best of luck and lots of success with your future work. If any of my friends have a need for a photographer, I will definitely tell them to call you. Sincere thanks." Aaron and Jessica S.

"Thank you so much for the pictures-we are really pleased with them. You did a wonderful job and most importantly for us made the grueling task of picture taking fun! Thanks again. I will wholeheartedly recommend you to friends if the opportunity arises." Yours, Lisa

"Thanks so much for the pictures. They were fantastic. Laura you have a great reference in me. Send some business cards and I'll send them to friends." Love, Terry & Ron

"David and I thank you so much for doing our photography at the wedding. The pictures turned out very nice. Thank you for being so patient." Joy & David

"Myron and I want to tell you how pleased we are with our wedding pictures. Everyone who sees them says they look beautiful. Thanks for all your great work which made our wedding day perfect. I hope to send some referrals your way." Myron & Maurine R.

"I just wanted to say thanks again for the wonderful job you did on Tracee's pictures. I've been showing the pictures at work and everyone is really pleased and surprised that they were done so quickly. Take care and thanks again." Jacqueline T.

"Thanks for the Christmas photos, they are wonderful! P.S. You are a great photo artist too! Love ya." Phyllis & Stan P

"Thank you again for all your patience and hard work. We really appreciate our job well done. I hope to refer many friends to you in the future. Sincerely." Greg and Dawn H

"It has been very nice working with you. Thanks a Bunch." Mary N.

"I got the pictures yesterday. They look great! Thank you so much." Leiloni.

"We feel that you were the key to our wedding being successful. Thanks for everything". Joe & Holly

"Thanks so much for the beautiful photos and memories!" Dee & John

"Thanks for photographing our wedding. You did a fantastic job! Merry Christmas." Love, Deb and Rod B

"Thank you for being so kind and so helpful. You are a gem." Marilyn S.

"You made me feel so at ease & the photos were awesome!" Sheila G.

CONTACT US & ORDERING PAGE

If you create a monthly E-newsletter, make the sign up process simple with person's name and email address. State that you will not sell or distribute the email to any third party. Make the order forms as simple as possible to fill in. This page should include a box where the sender has to type in the letters to avoid the robotic spam emails. If you have products to sell you will need a secure business credit card account to process orders on line.

7.5 Professional Business Card

Purchasing professionally printed business cards costs less than spending money on ink and paper to print off a home computer.

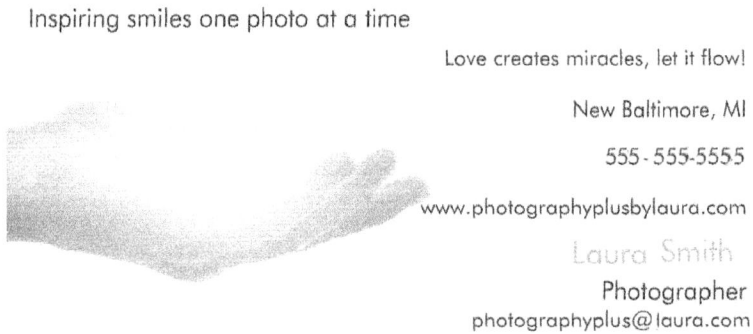

Vista Print Card example

The business card shown here came from **VistaPrint.com** They have a free card offer where the customer only pays for shipping, but the card has the Vista Print web address on the back. This makes the photographer look cheap and unprofessional. Your goal is to sell your service, so spend the little bit extra for cards without the printer's web address or logo on the back.[15]

And don't be shy about telling people what you do and passing out your business cards. When you're checking out at the grocery, hardware, or department store, when you pull out your credit card to pay, hand the clerk a card and say, "Thanks for helping me, I would like to give you one of my cards."

When dining out and you leave a nice tip for your food server, include a card. And don't forget about giving your friends, and other people you met a card. Plus use them as a calling card, the possibilities are endless.

7.6 The Wise Advertiser

When advertising be selective about where you chose to advertise. Because, once your business name begins appearing in the phone book, on the Internet, and on mailing lists, companies start calling you trying to sell you costly advertising gimmicks. It might not make you money, but the company selling you the gimmick will.

Ads on the backside of grocery receipts. People either look at their receipt before they leave the store or shove it into the bag and throw it away when they get home. If they do turn it over they spend about ten seconds looking at the back before tossing it into the trash.

Restaurant place mats ads. At the high end restaurants where people with money dine, I have never seen one of these placemats. I have seen them in the local mom and pop diners where the same patrons hang out and drink the bottomless cup of coffee. Since they are probably accustomed to seeing the placemats, I doubt many of those diners were calling the numbers or writing down the info. Need I say more?

Shopping cart purse and seat ads. Your target audience here is women because that is where they set their kids and purse which covers up the advertisement. And since woman are the

Clicking for Cash from Home   Laura L. Smith

ones who usually push the shopping cart—men will probably not be looking at the ad. And when someone does glance at the ad—it is for about five seconds before the person starts to shop or is leaving the store.

Park benches ads. One company I looked at had rates of $500 per ad per 4 week period—plus the buyer had to purchase a minimum of 10 to 50 bench advertisements. That can buy a lot of pens, business, and post cards.

The thick business bulk Ad envelops with coupons. When I worked as a mail sorter on automated sorting machinery, the envelope edges would get caught, ripping it open and tearing up the coupons. The torn coupons would be tossed into a tray to eventually be discarded. There went that businesses advertising money into the trash.

The sole photographer for an employee discount savings card. I fell for this one and admit I paid a non-refundable $650.00 fee to the Perks card to be the exclusive photographer for one year. Sad part was I never received one single call. On the anniversary date a sales representative called me back and asked if I wanted to renew and needless to say, I passed on that one. At least I was able to write off that fiasco on my taxes as an advertising expense.

The Cambridge Who's Who scam. A representative called and attempted to sell me a $600.00 plan that included having my name placed in a book, receiving an official certificate... a $100.00 gift certificate to a jewelry store I had never heard of and a free weekend at a time-share resort. Catch is I had to listen to a presentation about the resort. The authentic Who's Who in America was first published in 1899. It lists information on famous and notable Americans, not the average photographer working out of their home.

What I finally did go with was ink pens with my business name, web address, and phone number imprinted on the side and yearly calendars to give my clientele from **Pens.com**.

The Freedom of Social Media

Free or low cost social media resources to advertise can include LinkedIn, Twitter, Facebook, WordPress blogging and writing articles for online publications, sending email newsletters through Constant Contact or MailChimp, a Google site, and search engines.

One free advertising source is to create a one to two minute video or a drag and drop slide show of your business using the Pinnacle Studio's software. Then you can upload the video or slideshow to YouTube.

To create the video write or type out a two minute script in large face type letters that you can read from a distance. Then place a video camera on a tripod so you can record yourself reading the script.

If you have an assistant, have them hold the scrip up while you read it. If you are by yourself, cut the script into sections and tape it on different areas of the camera tripod or the wall behind the camera. The idea is to look as if you are not reading a script.

It is common when we speak for our eyebrows and the side of our mouth to droop. To remedy this, read the script with a smile and lift up your eyebrows. If you sit while recording you may have to lift your head slightly up to avoid the double chin affect.

Look directly at the camera lens and practice until you can read the script smoothly in audible tone of voice and without any mistakes.

Wear a nice shirt, slacks, and jacket. Record your video in front of blank or sitting at a clean and organized desk.

Another avenue to garner attention is entering juried photography competitions or having solo photo shows. It does cost money to prepare for venues like this, but it is free advertising. I never sold anything, but I did have people calling me to do photography work for them.

Phone Book advertising

Back in 1991 when I started my photography business—the trusty Qwest Dex yellow pages were a staple in people's homes. It was the main go to source to find a photographer. An advertiser had the option of choosing from the 1/16, 1/8, 1/4, 1/2, 3/4, or full page advertisement.

My first 1/16 Qwest Dex yellow page ad cost me $39.99 a month, which included my business name and phone number listing in the white pages.

When the availability and ease of the Internet and social media came into vogue, I scaled down to the bold two line ad with company name, website, and phone number in the white and yellow pages. And what I found was that the same amount of calls came in as when I had the 1/16 page advertisement. This proved to me that a larger ad did not mean more business.

I signed up for the Qwest Dex premiere on-line advertisement. When visitors clicked on the phone icon, it called my business. The ad also had a link to my website. The rate was $69.00 a month and I had to sign a non-refundable one year contract. At the end of the year I did not renew and opted for the free listing that were under the paid listings.

The free site option did not have the phone icon, only the website link. Surprisingly I ended up getting as many clicks on my website as I did when I paying for the premium ad.

In both the hardcopy phone book and the on-line site, some photography ads showed the PPA and the Kodak Symbol of Photography Excellence emblems. I once surveyed 20 people as part of a school project by showing them the two symbols and asked if they knew what they meant. The people had no idea and said they were more interested in how good a photographer's work looked and how much they charged.

However, for those who want that special certification, PPA.com offers a certification prep class which costs about $229.00 to obtain a Certified Master photographer designation, after taking the require courses. Depending upon the course and length it can cost $379.00 or more. If you join membership costs over $300.00 a year and you can set up a photographer page. The PPA also has a magazine you can subscribe too.

There is also the Kodak ProPass Premium Membership at **Findapro.kodak.com.**

7.7 Bridal Shows—No Profits for YOU!

Bridal show companies can charge anywhere from $175.00 to $325.00 for a six foot table. Plus add in the expenses of business cards, plan and pricing info sheets and brochures, a large bowl of candy or other treats for people visiting your table, a free drawing, pens, or DVD slide show samples and a bridal show can ends up being a costly investment.

I participated in four bridal shows over 20 years, and even though I stood out in front of the booth, smiled, talked to and gave people my information, and followed up with phone calls, I never got one job from a bridal show! Plus, neither did the people I knew such as a limo company owner, caterers, and DJ's. At one bridal show I assisted a friend with her chocolate fountain display and she did not receive one call, let alone a job.

At one show, I had my daughter survey 100 women on why they were attending and these were the top three responses:

- I paid to get in for the chance to win a free bridal gown
- I was looking for free gifts and food
- I went with a friend because I had nothing better to do

With stats like that, I probably would have been better off paying the admission, milling through the crowd, and discreetly handing out an ink pen along with a smile.

7.8 Photography Leads—it's the way to business

As a wedding photographer, you will need quality leads to find brides. The primary source most photographer s use is the pay-per-lead from a wedding based web site that has brides looking for services.

Additional resources to getting leads can be found using social media such as: being an affiliate with other wedding websites, offering special deals on your website, having a free photography blog at WordPress, writing photography articles on sites like Ezine that directs readers back to your website, and using the right promotional email to send a prospective client when you get a lead.

The promotional email template is available as part of the bonus promotion materials you receive for buying this book. (See Chap 8, page 122 for info on how to access yours).

When sending your email, use your name in the address line, i.e. Photo pricing from (your name). Notice how the email focuses on the prospective client with promises and a limited time premium offer after the P.S. When the recipient clicks on your website link—it should go to your home page also known as the landing page.

Hello (*email recipients name*)

Congratulations on your upcoming wedding!

My name is (*your name*) and my company is (*your company*). I received your information from (*friend/company*) and do have the (*date of event*) available to photograph your wedding.

At (Your Company) I or we believe in offering our clients affordable plans starting at (*$ amt to $ amt*) which includes:

- All the edited 4" x 6" prints in a white embossed wedding proof album

- A full resolution CD of all the images—great for sharing with family and friends

- A set of enlargements of your choice—depending upon the plan

Additionally (client's name) you will also receive at no additional cost…
- My exclusive black & white, sepia, hand tinting and photo painting features.

Plus, I also offer a complete line of flush mount enlargement albums, photo books, pillows, blankets and easy to use on-line ordering.

For complete pricing information please visit my web site at (*your website*) or call (*your number*) or reply back through this email.

Sincerely,

Your name, website, Phone (Place on separate lines.

P.S. And by the way (*recipient's name*), I wanted to let you know that *for this (year) only*—when you book the Standard, Deluxe, or Premier Plan…

When you place your album order you can chose
- ***$50.00*** off the parent's album regular **$475.00** listed price or
- ***$100.00*** off the Renaissance enlargement album regular **$650.00** listed price.

The Lead Sources
Here is a list of wedding sites where you can advertise and buy leads, but first…

Business Tip—my experience when visiting sites that had the phrase 'Please contact one of our representatives for pricing info,' usually equated to a high quote.

- **Blooming.briderush.com**—this website offers advertising plans for $19.99 a month.

- **Brideappeal.com/home**—this website is selling wedding marketing, SEO, & website design services.

- **Respond.com**—charged my account $5.00 every time someone clicked on the phone icon. My problem was the high school kids calling and asking questions for their class project.

- **Theknot.com** and the **Weddingchannel.com**—these two websites are part of the same group. When I inquired about pricing The Knot quoted me $69.00 a month to advertise on their site.

- **twitter.com/FreeWeddingLead**—If you use Twitter--interesting concept

- **Yourbridalplanner.com**—includes a vendor listing on this site, complete with cover photo, about paragraph and contact info, telephone, and link to your website.

- **Wedalert.com**—charges about $2 a lead, I used this one.

There are also web sites where photography businesses bid for the top spot. This turns into a competition and the bids can go up to a dollar or more a day.

7.9 Free link exchange wedding sites

These are also known as reciprocal sites. The concept is that when you sign up, the other site will list your website in exchange for placing their banner on one of your website pages.

On the **wedj.com/dj** link to us page, this site has twelve different styles of banners. This one banner shows how it will appear on a website page [16]

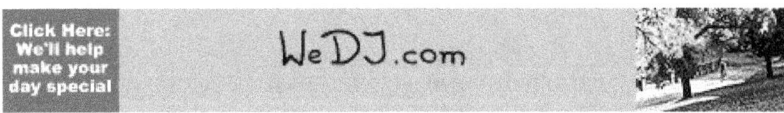

Underneath each banner is the html code that creates the banner on your website:

<A HREF="http://www.wedj.com"><IMGSRC="http://www.wedj.com/dj-photo-video.nsf/wedjbanner7.gif?Open ImageResource"WIDTH=468HEIGHT=60 ALT="Find a DJorPhotographeratWeDJ.com"BORDER=0></A>

Here is what to do to place another sites link on your website.

First open your text editor tool of the page you want to place the banner. The text editor will create the hyperlink back to the other site.

Cut and paste one of the other sites banners html code into the section of your Business links page, or other page, where you want it to appear.

This requires scrolling down and looking for the html code that has the website name in the first line i.e. *<A HREF="http://www.joanscakecreations"><IMGSRC=* of the item above where you are going to insert the hyperlink. Then paste in the html code on the next line under the ad.

Do not paste the html code directly onto the web page as copy, it will not link back.

When listing your website on a reciprocal site, add the website page after the .com. For example the link should look like: *www.janesphotography.com/links.* This shows the reciprocal site where you placed their banner.

If you type in just your web site name with no specific page after the .com/ the site will ask for the page.

Here are three other reciprocal websites:

- **weddingblogs100.com/advertise-with-us.html**

- **mywedding.com/apps/public/content/advertising**

- **allseasonsweddings.com/wedding-link-exchange**

7.10 Search optimizing engines (SEO)

Once you are advertising your business on-line—you likely will receive emails and calls from companies trying to sell you're their "search engine optimizing" or SEO services. The following is an example of the typical sales call from a SEO representative:

"Hello, is this Laura, the owner of Photograph Plus by Laura? Well good morning Laura. My name is CON JOB and I want to let you know that recently I did an Internet search for your website and noticed that you are not listed on most of the major search engines and directories. Are you aware, Laura, that you are losing business because of this? Well I am glad that I was able to make you aware of that and would like to help you. Are you aware that our company *We Steal You Blind*, is a top ranked search engine optimization service that works in partnership with *Google, Yahoo, Bing*, and all the other search engines to give you a #1 ranking at the top of those sites for only $19.99 dollars a month, which is a small investment to direct more clients to your website. How does that sound Laura? I would love to sign you up today to get those paying clients to your site".

I then would politely decline the offer because according to Google: *"**No one can guarantee a #1 ranking on Google.** Beware of SEOs that claim to guarantee rankings, allege a "special relationship" with Google, or advertise a "priority submit" to Google. There is no priority submit for Google. In fact, the only way to submit a site to Google directly is through our Add URL page or by submitting a Sitemap and you can do this yourself at no cost whatsoever"*[17] (Google 2014).

Then I asked Con Job, "Oh so as long as I type my business name with the city and state in the search bar, I will be ranked number one with all the search engines, right? Con Job began to give me further rhetoric and I said, no thank you and hung up.

But you don't have to pay an SEO service for something you can do yourself for free.

The way a search engine works is computers send out spiders that crawl out to billions of web pages on the Internet. It is an algorithmic process where a computer program determines which sites to crawl to, how often, and how many pages to take from each site. Then the spider processes each page to compile an index of keywords it sees and the location on each page.

So when you use Google, Yahoo, or Bing to do an Internet search, those sites use their computers to search their indexes for matching pages and return the results most relevant to the user. Google relevancy is determined by over 200 factors.

There are legitimate SEO companies out there, but you need to ask the right questions. The following questions is from the Google WebMaster Tools help site[18]

- Can you show me examples of your previous work and share some success stories?
- Do you follow the Google Webmaster Guidelines?
- Do you offer any online marketing services or advice to complement your organic search business?
- What kind of results do you expect to see, and in what timeframe? How do you measure your success?
- What's your experience in my industry?
- What's your experience in my country/city?
- What's your experience developing international sites?
- What are your most important SEO techniques?
- How long have you been in business?
- How can I expect to communicate with you? Will you share with me all the changes you make to my site, and provide detailed information about your recommendations and the reasoning behind them?[18] (Google 2014).

To use the SEO website verification on a WordPress site, click on tools on the left side bar in the dashboard to open the tool page. Then scroll down to the Website Verification services. Next click on each of the Google, Bing, Pinterest, Twitter, and Yandex links and follow the instructions.

If your website is through another company, they are probably already using SEO for their clients. Even if your website is built from scratch, you don't have to hire a SEO service. You can got to Google WebMaster optimization and do your own.

 First you have to open a Google account, log in, and go to **Google WebMaster Tools**. Then you click on the red **ADD A SITE** button. A box will pop up and you type in your web site URL then click continue. Another page will pop up asking you to verify your ownership of your website. Click on the red **verify button** at the bottom and follow the instructions.

You can also click on the Alternate methods box and click on the HTML tag which will give you a Meta tag you can cut and paste into your website text editor under Meta Tags. Or you can click on the HTML file upload and follow the instructions.

You can also attract the spiders by typing in SEO key words into your Meta tags text editor of your website. The keywords I used were: *wedding photographers, wedding photography, event photographers, Detroit wedding and event photographers, Michigan wedding photographers, portrait photographer, Bar-bat mitzvah photographers, quinceanera photography, pet photography, Detroit commercial photographers*, etc. Make sure to type in your city and state.

7.11 Online Viewing—Keep the Client Clicking

Back in the day, photography studios would emboss the studio name in gold in a lower bottom corner of proofs and placed them into proof folders. The client would set an appointment to come to the studio to view the proofs and place an order. Today, most studios and photographers use online viewing and ordering of weddings and events because:

1) No money is spent on printing the proofs and buying a proof album

2) The client(s) can't scan the proof into their computer to email or print out

3) It keeps the client clicking their mouse to order photos

Even if a photographer has a low fee to shoot the wedding or event—they can still make a lot of money with online ordering.

Case in point: I once receive a call from a woman to come to her home and show her how to order on-line photos of her son's graduation party. The photographer had only charged $175.00 for the two hour session and there were 200 photos. The reprint pricing was: a 4" x 6"—$5.50… a 5" x 7"—$9.00… an 8" x 10"—$15.00 and an 11" x 14"—$30.00.

When she chose an enlargement, the photo popped up and she had to crop it. It took 1.5 hours to crop and order. The woman got so caught up in ordering that at the end the total came to just over $850.00 and she paid it by credit card.

Online viewing and ordering is okay but because I offered hardcopy prints too, clients hired me over the competition many times over. Client's liked that they received all the photos plus they had the option of on-line ordering. Plus, I still got enlargement reorders as my pricing was affordable.

Here is a list of online sites for uploading wedding or other event jobs for online viewing by the client.

Photostockplus.com—I opted for the yearly payment plan and printed out on card stock paper the following information so the bride could pass on the cards to family members:

For on line ordering: *Your username.Photostockplus.com.* Password: *Brides first name or visit (Photographers website)* and go to Photography services and click on the link at the top of the page.

- **Collages.net**
- **Shutterfly.com**
- **Photoproofpro.com**
- **Digiproofs.com**
- **Shootproof.com**
- **Imagequix.com**
- **Pictage.com**
- **Picturespro.com**
- **Zenfolio.com**

Most of sites listed above also offer canvas prints, cups, key rings, and other gift items. However, I found it easier to order through Sams Club photo service because I could pick it up from the store, instead of having to pay for shipping.

Chapter 8 PROMOTIONAL PRODUCTS

You are entitled to receive free—all the word documents templates featured in this guide. All you need do is email laural.s2012@gmail.com. Please include your name, email, and where you purchased the book.

8.1 Promotional Photo Items

For the customer photo books, I used **MyPublisher.com** and added on a minimal profit. There are other photo book publishers, such as **Collages.net** that also offer gallery wraps, cards, and story blocks.

To showcase your scenic and stock photography there is self publishing at **Create Space**, a division of Amazon. It will be assigned an ISBN number and will be available for sale to the public. Therefore, be careful not to use your client's photos.

For example let's say you create a B & W photo book with text and price it retail at $14.99, the author cost might be $4.44 a book. And since it is a print on demand (POD) publisher, you can order as little or as many books you want or need. The price is much less than ordering through a self publishing book company, like Morris Publishing, that requires the author to buy a certain amount of books.

Photo Sheet

The photo sheet is a great marketing tool to mail and/or give to the client at the end of an interview.

The 8" x 10" proof sheet shown on the next page was easy to create by using the **FongSoft** program which is downloaded into Photoshop 7.0 and higher. It is available at **GaryFongstore.com.** Now if you do not want to spend the money buying Photoshop--**Adobe.com** has a 30 day free trial.

After opening the **FongSoft** program, you can chose nine to thirty photos to be dropped and dragged onto the sheet, but I found that nine photos worked best. You can also type in your business name, website, and phone number. The **FongSoft** program is also used to create flush mount photo layouts.

If you do not have the **FongSoft** program, you can make a photo sheet using Microsoft word.

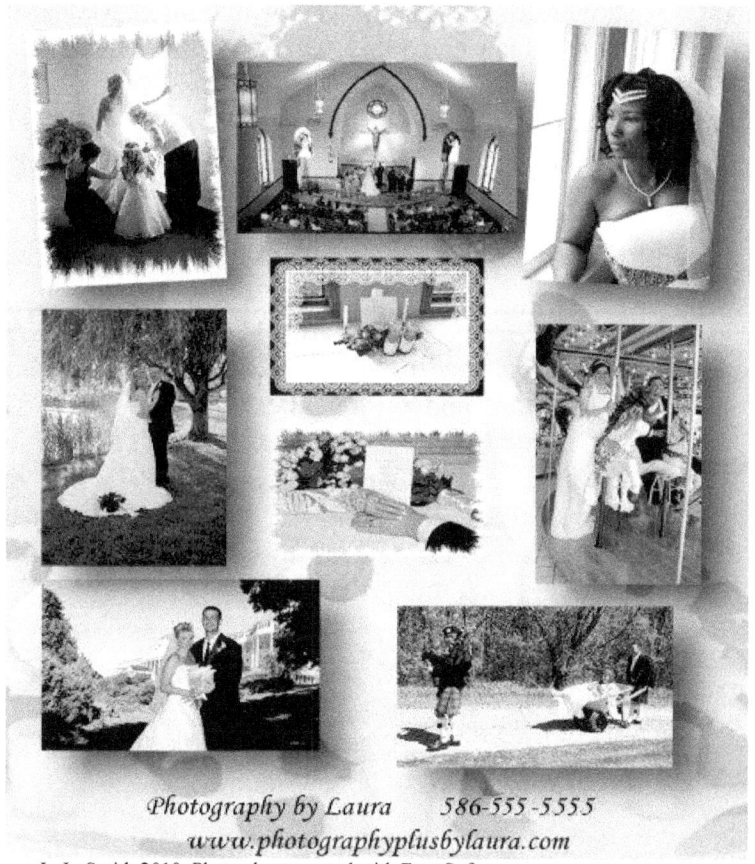

Photography by Laura   586-555-5555
www.photographyplusbylaura.com
L. L. Smith 2010 Photo sheet created with FongSoft

1. Make a new folder and chose up to nine of your best photos. Copy them and past them place them into the new folder. This way you save your original photo.

2. Then open the first photo in the folder in Microsoft Office Picture Manager, choose the editing resize tool and click on the Go to Predefined width x height drop down box. This will resize the photo to 1024 x 768 px. Save the photo and move to the next one until all photos are resized.

3. Next open a word document and start inserting the photos. They will show up large and you will have to reduce the photos by moving a corner to the size you want.

4. Once all the photos are on the page, click on the first one and it should go to the page layout options. Click on the text wrapping icon and a box will drop down. Chose the square option and click on it. This will give you the ability to move the photo around on the page. Do the same with the rest of the photos and arrange the photos the way you want.

5. Then add your text at the bottom and save the document.

8.2 The Brochure—Simple, Effective & Attractive

I designed a front and back paged, three fold services brochure using Microsoft word and printing it at a copy center. The brochure was made in the portrait layout and featured the Monotype Corsiva, Edwardian Script ITC, and Times New Roman typefaces, red, black, and blue for colors, and a page border of hearts. It did not contain my price list as I wanted the potential client to call me for pricing.

Front side of brochure
First Section
Since 2000 (*Edwardian Script ITC size 28*)
(*Writing below was done in times new roman 12 point in green*)
(your company name) has provided affordable quality for her clients.
(Your name) is an experienced and dedicated photographer who captures your special and important moments with a knowledgeable, personable, and professional attitude.
(Your name) also provides:
- Up front pricing with no hidden fees
- Timely turnaround of your photos
- Complementary touch-ups
- No extra fees for black and white and sepia photography
- Weddings: All your 4" x 6" prints in a beautiful proof album, full resolution CD and enlargements
- On line viewing & ordering
- No copyright or proof markings on your photos

Second section
Website Phone Email (Times New Roman 12. Centered with three lines in bold)

Third Section
Photography by Your Company Phone: 555-555-5555 your website name (*Edwardian Script ITC size 28*)
Creating Smiles One Photo at a Time (Monotype Corsiva size 22)

<u>Back side of flyer</u>:
First section
Photography by Laura (large sized Edwardian Script ITC)

Second Section
Services and Products: (Edwardian Script ITC size 48)
(*The following was done in Times New Roman 14*)
- **Weddings**
- **Bar-bat mitzvahs**
- **Anniversaries and Birthdays**
- **Engagement photos, seniors, & pets**
- **Baby and Wedding Showers**
- **Wedding Albums & DVD slide shows**
- **Corporate and Special Events**
- **On location portraits**
- **Decorative photo artwork**
- **Photo restoration and editing**
- **Photo blankets and pillows**
- **Large prints up to 30" x 40"**

Third Section
When only the best will do for you photographic needs (*Times New Roman size 28*)

8.3 Promotional Informational Sheets

Years ago, an acquaintance who worked for a well known stock brokerage firm, told me that he used fear, uncertainty, and fear or F.U.D. as a sales technique. He said this was how he got prospective clients to buy investment and insurance products.

Now, myself, I don't ascribe to the philosophy of using fear to get clients. Instead, I prefer to elicit trust in clients by providing timely information to assure them I'm the right photographer for the job. In this section I discuss and provide the informational sheets I gave to prospective clients when I met with them.

The PREPS of Photography
Professionalism, Reliability, Experience, Price, and Service

When choosing a photographer for your special day you want to be sure that the service is professional and your photographs will be there for you. This informational sheet can help you ask the right questions of a photographer to insure that your wedding day will be a beautiful reminder in photographs and not a disastrous loss.

- **Professionalism**: Does the photographers web site showcase only about 20 to 25 of their best wedding photos in a slow moving slideshow set to music? Or is there a variety of formal, creative, candid, and spontaneous photos that showcases the different aspects of a wedding event? Is the photographer nice, cheerful, attentive, flexible, and helpful? Or is the photographer egotistical, haughty and knows what is best for you?

- **Reliability**: Does the photographer have a history of being late to appointments or events? Can the photographer deliver your photos, albums, CD, or DVD slide shows within a reasonable time period such as one month vs. six months? Does the photographer back up your work on a CD right after the wedding so it is not lost if his/her CF card or PC crashes?

- **Compliance**: How is your personal information protected? Is on a password protected computer with up to date antivirus software? Does anyone else in the photographer's family or other business associates have access to the photographer's computer? Are the client's sensitive information and or wedding on a portable flash drive the photographer is carrying all over the place? Is the photographer leaving his lap top with your sensitive information and photos in the front seat of his car in plain sight making it vulnerable to theft?

- **Experience**: The better choice is to hire the experienced home based photographer who is the one who shoots one to two weddings a week—rather than a random studio photographer who does maybe one a month.

- **Price**: The studio store front photographer charging $3500.00 to $7500.00 to cover overhead, does not mean better. The lower priced photographer who works out of their home can do just as good a job at a better value.

- **Service**: Does the photographer return your phone calls and emails in a timely manner? Are they flexible and willing to work with you on staying within in your budget? Will they accommodate your photography requests? Are they the photographer that will be photographing your wedding or do they send someone else?

Additionally, the photographer you hire should have a varied portfolio... be well trained and experienced both in photography and business techniques... have great communication skills... love what they do and enjoy working with their clients.

Wedding Service Informational Sheet

Photography by Your Company
Creating Smiles one Photo at a Time
Web site: **yourcompany@abc.com**
Your email
Phone: 555-555-5555
Mission statement: To provide affordable and quality photography

Events I photograph
- Weddings
- Bar-bat mitzvahs
- School groups
- Sports teams
- Portraits & Large groups
- Architecture
- Reunions
- Corporate functions
- Art work
- Food & Jewelry
- Pets & Animals
- Anniversary & birthday parties

Products
- DVD album shows
- Coffee table books
- Sports photo cards
- Matted & flush mount albums
- Photo blankets & pillows
- Mini wallet flush mount album

(Your) Achievements—*(I use mine as an example)*
- 2007—Honorable Mention—Photography Competition
- 2007—June Artist of the Month
- 2006—Solo October Artist of the Month,

- 2006—Best of American Artists book by Kennedy Productions
- 2006—Photo Forum Best of Annual Photography
- 2006—December issue of Detroit Style magazine
- 2006—International photography exhibition
- 2006—Photos featured in Opera House New Years Gala
- 2005—Michigan All media juried exhibition
- 2005—Greeting card line featured at Art Gallery
- 1998—Department of Tourism 7th place winner

The advantages of trusting (your company name)
- All services and pricing is upfront, no hidden fees
- All touch ups, black & white, sepia and photo painting is included in all packages
- I can change out backgrounds
- I offer online ordering of your event
- I back up all photo files onto CD
- There are no copyright marks on the photos, CDs, or DVD album shows. The client can email and share their photos with family and friends. No more wasted time scanning and editing hard copy photos.
- I am the one who shows up—not someone else
- Timely turnaround time of no more than a week and a half
- I offer one day service on reprints and enlargements under 20" x 30" plus postage is included in all mail orders.
- Ala cart pricing—buy only what you want.
- I use a bounce flash diffuser which creates a depth of field instead of the flattened look of direct flash and eliminates shadows around the head and body area.

8.4 The Perceived Value of Pricing

The key to a pricing schedule is to create perceived value.

I created my pricing sheet to make the client think he was receiving a better deal over the competition. This was done by using the words **ultimate, premier, deluxe**, and **standard** instead of numbers to label the plans. Plus, I only listed four plans with the top plan first followed by the lesser plans.

The idea was to make it simple for the client to make a choice. Too many plans are confusing and you risk losing the client.

The pricing sheet also listed the Ala Carte services that was not so much there for people to buy from—but used to show the client how much value they were receiving in the plans.

For example The Ultimate Plan is $2500.00 and has an engagement session—a **$125.00** value. It also includes 7 to 9 hours, 300—4" x 6" prints in proof album and the CD. The Premier Plan is $1275.00 and includes 9 hours and the same amount of prints, the proof album, and CD. So that **$1275.00** value is added onto the Ultimate plan.

The Ultimate Plan also includes an album choice— **$675.00** value. A 16" x 20" frame print—**$135.00** value and a coffee table book **$135.00**.

We then add up these values for a total of **$2345.00**. So when the client looks at the Ultimate plan, then adds up the extras— the perceived values is—why not pay the extra **$1225.00** upgrade for the Ultimate Plan for all the extras. (Good thing the client **doesn't know what your low wholesale cost** is).

The second part is listing your expenses and then adding your worth to equal a profit. The following is an expense schedule to consider in setting a pricing schedule.

- Editing: 350 wedding photos may take 24 hours to edit depending upon computer speed, breaks, and photo effects.

- Travel time, mileage, fuel, and insurance

- Photo printing costs, proof albums, enlargements if included with the plan

- Phone book advertising, lead costs, home and cell phone and internet costs.

- Ink and paper costs to print out flyers, price and brochure sheets, and wedding agreements.

- Credit card machine, business banking fees and tax preparation fees

- Replacing worn out sync cords, batteries cables, hot shoe adapters, plus buying new cameras and software.

Pricing and Agreement Forms
Wedding Pricing Sheet
Company Name
Since XXXX—Creating Happy Smiles with Beautiful and Quality Photography
555-123-4567 555-233-5555
E-mail:
Address
Web site:

No additional charges for touch ups, black and white, sepia, and photo tinting
I offer online ordering of reprints, enlargements, and photo gifts.
I do not require photographer only rights so family and friend are welcome to take photos too.

Ultimate Plan $2500.00 Includes: 7 to 9 hours. Engagement photo session with CD. 300—4" x 6" prints in proof album & CD. An album of ___ 12-8" x 10"s & 24-5" x 7"s or ___ flush mount album of 10 pages, 20 sides. A 16" x 20" framed photograph and coffee table book.

Premier Plan $1275.00—9 hours: Over 300-4"x6" prints in album, 10-8"x10"s, 8-5"x7"s, & photo CD.

Deluxe Plan $1075.00—6 hours: Up to 300-4"x6" prints in album, 8-8"x10"s , 6-5"x7"s, & photo CD

Standard Plan $825.00—4 hours: Up to 275-4"x6" prints in album, 4-8"x10"s, 6-5"x7"s, & photo CD.

Ala Carte Extras:
- Engagement session.. $125.00
- Photo light & back drop..................................... $ 50.00
- Enlargement Album. 12—8" x 10"s & 24—5" x 7".. $675.00
- Art Leather Flush mount album-10 pages, 20 sides $675.00
- Parents Album. 24-5" x 7"s.............................. $299.00
- Framed 16" x 20" framed enlargement................... $135.00
- Woven Photo Blanket 54" x 70"-Your photo choice... $125.00

- Photo pillow- (Your choice of photo)................. $ 40.00
- DVD Slide show... $125.00
- Leather or linen coffee table book (15 pgs/30 sides).. $135.00
- Digital brag books (15 pgs/ 30 sides)............... $ 39.99

Reprint and Enlargement pricing:

- 4" x 6".........$ 2.25
- 5" x 7".........$ 5.50
- 8" x 10"........$12.50
- 11" x 14"......$25.00

- 16" x 20".......$45.50
- 20" x 30".......$65.00

Product and Enlargement Pricing Sheet Example

Company Name
Providing affordable & quality photography since XXXX
Phone: 555-555-5555
Cell: 555-555-555
E-mail: your email
Website

Studio enlargement pricing of $30.00 for an 8" x 10" or $1200.00 for an enlargement album is just too much to pay!

Instead save with my discounted savings on enlargements, albums, DVD slide shows, and photo pillows.

You also save time ordering by emailing your digital files on CD to me—No more driving to the store to pick up your photos. Plus—postage is included in the pricing.
List below are my Ala Carte services. To see examples please Visit my web site to view examples of products listed below.

Enlargements:
- 8" x 10".. $12.50
- 11" x 14"... $25.00
- 16" x 20"... $45.50
- 20" x 30"... $65.00

The Milano Renaissance Matted Album:
- Includes 12—8" x 10"s & 24-5" x 7"s.......... $495.00
Art Leather Albums:
- Parents Album: includes 24—5" x 7"s.......... $299.00
- Flush Mount Album—10 pages, 20 sides $595.00

Other Products:
- Leather & Linen cover books.......$135.00—Up to 30 pages
- Digital Paperback Brag books..............$40.00--20 pages
- Digital DVD slide show of your event........... $85.00
- Extra DVD copies................................... $10.00
- Photo pillows... $45.00

Photography Agreement Form Example

Photography by (Your Company Name & Event) Photography Agreement

Please make checks payable to (Your Company Name)

I, _____ have hired **Your Company Name**
for _____ on (date)_____time _____
Address/directions_____
_____

____$250.00 deposit paid.

___**Ultimate Plan** $2500.00—Includes 7 to 9 hours. Engagement photo session with CD. 300—4" x 6" prints in proof album & CD. An album of ___ 12-8" x 10"s & 24-5" x 7"s or ___ flush mount album of 10 pages, 20 sides. A 16" x 20" framed photograph and coffee table book..

___ **Premier Plan** $1275.00—9 hours: Over 300-4"x6" prints in album, 10-8"x10"s, 8-5"x7"s, & photo CD.

___ **Deluxe Plan** $1075.00—6 hours: Up to 300-4"x6" prints in album, 8-8"x10"s , 6-5"x7"s, & photo CD

___ **Standard Plan** $825.00—4 hours: Up to 275-4"x6" prints in album, 4-8"x10"s, 6-5"x7"s, & photo CD.

Ala carte:
- ___ Engagement session................................... $125.00
- ___ Photo light & back drop............................... $ 50.00
- ___ Enlargement Album. 12—8" x 10"s & 24—5" x 7". $675.00
- ___ Art Leather Flush mount album-10 pages, 20 sides $675.00
- ___ Parents Album. 24-5" x 7"s............................$299.00
- ___ Framed 16" x 20" framed enlargement................ $135.00
- ___ Woven Photo Blanket 54" x 70"-Your photo choice $125.00

__ Photo pillow- (Your choice of photo)................. $ 40.00
__ DVD Slide show.. $125.00
__ Leather or linen coffee table book (15 pgs/30 sides).. $135.00
__ Digital brag books (15 pgs/ 30 sides)............... $ 39.99

Deposits are non refundable if client cancels a week after the booking.

- Last day cancellations-Full price will be paid to Photography by Laura
- Photography by Laura is not held responsible for and from any injuries and or damages due to children and/or guests running into or tripping over photographer's equipment. If the photographer equipment is damaged by the clients, guests or their children— they shall be responsible for replacing the equipment with the same product or cash equivalent.
- If photos do not turn out, not due to photographers fault such as defective processing, lost or stolen, fire, or acts of God, all monies minus expenses shall be returned.

No refunds once client has examined the photographs, paid, and left the premises with photographs.

_____Date_____
Client signature

_____City _____Zip____
Client address

Telephone no. (___)_____Cell _____Email _____

Company name
Business address
Phone: 555-555-5555
Email: yourcompany@abc.com
website

All Purpose Event Agreement

Event Photography Agreement

Please make checks payable to (Your Company Name)

I,_____ have hired **Your Company Name**

for _____ on (date)_____time _____

Address/directions_____

_____

__ $375.00: Two hours. Includes 72—4" x 6" prints.

___ $250.00—Deposit paid

Photography by Laura is not held responsible for and from any injuries and or damages due to children and/or guests running into photographer's equipment.

No refunds shall be given once client has examined the photographs, paid, and left the premises with the photographs.

_____Date_____
Client signature
_____City _____Zip_____
Client address

Telephone no. (____) _____Cell _____Email_____

Company name
Business address
Phone: 555-555-5555
Email: yourcompany@abc.com
website

Chapter 9 WEDDINGS & EVENTS

Weddings and events will likely be the core revenue generators for your business. This chapter discusses protecting your profits and time management.

9.1 Keeping up your Profit Base

Wedding and events are money makers, so why risk losing your hard earned profit. But with some planning and following the steps presented here, you can avoid being taken advantage of so you don't flush your money down the drain.

SET A TIME LIMIT

It might seem redundant at this point, but no matter how anxious you are to get work, set time limits.

My first business ad was in the newspaper wedding services section. When I received a call to photograph a wedding, I was so focused on getting the job that I quoted a price of $525.00, but did not specific a time limit. I ended up at the event for 12 hours and took eight rolls of 24 exposure film. Needless to say I was exhausted and restructured my entire package pricing after that fiasco.

NO OVERTIME FEES

In the beginning I had on my agreement form, an overtime fee of $50.00 an hour which included up to 36—4" x 6" prints.

I had met with a bride-to-be who stated she was on a tight budget, but still wanted to hire me for my $925.00 six hour plan. She asked if I could lower my price $150.00 and I politely declined. She then opted for the four hour $725.00 plan and I gave her the agreement form to sign.

"Oh I see you have an overtime clause." she said. The OT option read: $50.00 an hour.

"Oh, okay, well I am going to check it just in case. I'm not saying definitely I might need you, but just in case." She said as she put a checkmark on the line.

I was oblivious to what she was planning at the time.

At the reception when my 10:00 p.m. end time came, the bouquet and garter toss had not been done. The woman then approached me and asked me to stay two more hours.

"I'm sorry but I can't stay." I replied.

"Well you have to stay, because when I checked the overtime option, you agreed to it by accepting the contract. And if you don't I don't have to pay you anything." She blurted out over the loud music.

It was then I realized I had been duped and was furious. But I stayed calm and said okay and she walked away. I ended up staying the entire two hour and shooting two more rolls of 36 exposure film for only a $100.00 more.

When the photos were ready to be picked up, the woman sent her mother with a check. When I began opening the box to take out the album, she said she didn't have the time to look at the photos. I then took the check, and gave the woman the photos and negatives and she left. Three days later, I got a call from the bride. She told me she was upset because forty of the photos were of poor quality and unusable and wanted me to refund her $100.00.

"Well according to the contract since you didn't come personally to examine the photos before leaving the premises, I don't owe you any refund." I said. A silence ensued.

"This isn't the end of this you should know!" She said and hung up. I never heard another word from her.

After that I removed the overtime option from my agreement form. From that point on when I was asked how much it would cost for me to stay an extra hour, I quoted $150.00. That ended that discussion right then and there.

CAN YOU CUT YOUR PRICE IF...?

From the beginning of my photography business, I would get the occasional "bargain shopper bride" calling and asking...

"If I don't want the prints and album how much less would your (name of) package be?"

When I shot with film, my cost for film, developing and printing plus the proof album was about $121.00. Even though the photos were edited at the processing lab, I was not about to give away my hard earned money.

When I told the 'bargain shopper bride' it would only be $50.00 less, she was surprised. She thought the price would be at least half off. Needless to say I was not hired.

When I began shooting digital, 'bargain shopper brides' would call asking, "if I just want the DVD, how much less will it be for the (name of) package?"

But because I was spending 24 hours editing 300 photos, the caller was informed "I'm sorry but I don't offer discounts".

The 'bargain shopper bride' would say, "oh, okay, thank you for your time," and hung up.

Bottom line: **You're worth every penny you make, don't' give it away.**

CONTRACTS

People can be unpredictable and cause you problems. That is why thorough documentation should always be included on your agreement form to protect you from anything that might be a problem. Because if it isn't documented, it wasn't done.

Always make sure both the future bride and groom signs the contract, even if the future bride shows up alone to the appointment. Have her take the agreement form home with a SASE so the fiancé can sign it and mail it back to you.

One time I had a bride who only signed the contract. Two months after the wedding she left the husband, filed bankruptcy and did not pick up the photos. I filed a claim against her ex-husband in small claims court to get my money.

I found out in court that the ex-husband was not responsible for payment because he did not sign the agreement form and was not in procession of the photos. Needless to say I was out the rest of my money sans the down payment.

I had another bride who hired me to photograph an outdoor wedding at noon time. I showed her midday photo examples and explained that bright sunlight washes out colors plus creates harsh shadows on the faces. She assured me there would be shade. I wrote a brief note on the agreement form, and we both dated it.

On the day of the wedding, there was no shade and I expressed my concern. She said it would be okay. When the photos were ready she had me meet her at a store parking lot where she paid and took the photos without looking at them.

Three days later she called and said she was devastated that everyone's faces had shadows on them and that all the colors were washed out. Plus since she had taken her bridal smile off right after the formal wedding photos, she looked horrible in the photos with her husband.

I apologized and reminded her that she had initialed the documentation that there would be shade provided. She then said that did not matter because I had caused her emotional trauma and she was going to contact her attorney to sue me for business fraud.

I said "Okay, I'm sorry you are traumatized, but you have no legal grounds for a refund due to mental distress".

"Yes I do, and you are going to pay me back my money!" She said and hung up. I never received another call from her.

I photographed a woman's parent's anniversary party which included an 11" x 14" and the negatives per the agreement form. A month after the event, the woman called to order the 11" x 14", I said for her to mail me the negative. Two weeks later I received a typed letter asking that I send the woman a check for $26.50 in a timely manner. She had enclosed a photocopied receipt from a photo lab showing an 11" x 14" and 2—5" x 7"s that had been printed and paid for.

I called her and explained I did not owe her the money. She said that she didn't feel comfortable mailing her only negative and there was no way that I could get an 11" x 14" for less than what she had paid. I repeated she could mail me the negative and I would have the 11" x 14" printed and mailed to her.

"Well it's obvious I am not going to get anywhere with you." she said and hung up.

In conclusion: **always document, date, and have the client sign the contract.** It can save you a lot of financial pain.

9.2 Wedding Day Time Management

The photographers wedding day time management goal is to keep things as stress free and smooth moving as they can. When I first started out I did not have a time line information sheet to give my client's. That all changed after I did a Catholic Church wedding with a strict two hour time limit.

The bride wanted studio lighting for the formal photos. She assured me I would have 35 minutes to take photos. However, the wedding started 15 minutes late, the ceremony was an over an hour, it took 15 minutes for the 400 guests to exit the church, plus the coordinator would not let me set up my studio lights when there were still people in the church.

This left 15 minutes to take a few flash photos, which was okay by the bridal couple, before people starting coming in for the afternoon confession time. She apologized for the late start time. When I got back the photos, because of the window light in the church the flash photos looked fine. When she came to look and pick up her photos, she was surprised they turned out as good as they did. She paid me and left. Incidentally, the next time I was called about photographing another wedding in that church, I passed.

9.3 Pre-Wedding and the ceremony time line

This time frame can vary from one to two hours. It is recommended that you plan to arrive a half hour at the ceremony location to give you time to meet and greet and assemble your equipment. The list below is a time guideline to help you plan your day.

- **Pre-wedding photos—*1.5 to 2.0 hours***: This is if the bridal couple wants photos of them getting dressed at the ceremony location, separate photos of the bride, bridesmaids, her family, and the groom, groomsmen and his family. Plus this time should cover people who are running late.

- **Late ceremony start times—*5 to 10*** minutes late.

- **Ceremony—*25 minutes to an hour***

- **Receiving line at the church—*15 to 20 minutes***

- **Signing the marriage license—*10 to 15 minutes***

- **On site formal photos—*35 to 40 minutes***: Depending on the amount of people, if everyone is present and not having to send out people to search for the absent ones.

- **Bustling the dress, bridal party photo by limo and driving to ceremony—*15 minutes to an hour***: Time length depends how fast the person bustles the dress... the wedding party knows to assemble for the limo photo and if the bridal party decides to drive around.

- **Off site formal photos—*1.0 to 1.5 hours***: Time length depends how soon the group arrives at the location... how quickly everyone gets out of the limo and assembles for the photos... and how much moving from place to another.

9.4 Posing the Formal Photos

After the ceremony people want to get to the reception. You should aim for a 35 minute time period for taking the formal photos. This may seem like an impossible goal, but if you practice on your own time using a list of the photos you need to take, you will find after a few weddings how efficiently your photographing will move along.

Unless you have the talent of remembering everyone's names, the best method is to call out for people by saying "I need the bride's parents, or the bride's family, etc." People may be talking and milling about. Other family members will be taking photos. Block it out and keep moving. Use the maid of honor to position and fluff out the bridal dress.

All large family group photos should be full length body shots instead of close ups. A close up of the parents with the bride and groom is fine, but also take full length body shots.

And always say, 1, 2, 3 smile, don't blink, take two photos of each group, and when done ask, have I gotten everyone? Anybody else here want a photo with the bride and groom?

Here is an efficient time saving order to take the photos:

- **Position the bride** on the right and the groom on the left facing you. Adjust the bottom of the brides dress so people will not be stepping on it.

- **First**— Pose the parents and grandparents in this standing sequence: father, mother, bride, groom and/or grandparents, parents, bride, groom, parents, grandparents. Then photograph the bride and her parents, then the grandparent's and bride, then both sets with bride. Next photograph the groom and his parents, then grandparent's and him. Then both sets with groom.

- **Second**—Photograph the bride's entire family. Offer mints as a reward to the small kids to cooperate. Then photograph the smaller family groups if requested.

141

- **Third**—Photograph the grooms entire family and smaller family groups.

- **Fourth**—The bridal party. First photograph the bride by herself, full front, back and face close-up, then individual photos with the maid of honor and bridesmaids and then a full group shot. Next photograph the groom's side in the same order.

- **Fifth**—The bridal couple. Position and photograph them with their arms around each other holding the bouquet in front. Then move up and take the ring hands on the bouquet. Set the bouquet aside. Next...
    - Take two close ups of the face move back and take...
    - Two face to the waist shots... then
    - Two full length body shots...
    - Then position the groom behind the bride with his hands around her waist and repeat the photo sequence above.
    - Then pose the couple facing each other and take a full length shot. Move up and squat down to take a photo of the groom kissing the brides forehead. Then stand up and take another photo. Then shoot any requests.

- **Sixth**—Photos of the gown being pinned up, the bridal party out by the limo and the bride and groom getting in.

If the bridal party takes an hour limo ride before arriving at the reception venue—this gives you time to take photos of the guests sitting at the tables, cake and gift tables, decorations, and any other family photos.

9.5 The Reception Time Line

At a reception the guests, other than family and close friends, stay about two hours. This includes the time they have already been waiting for the bridal party to show up. So, when meeting with the future bride and groom—here are two suggestions that I found most couples liked and performed.

The first one is to suggest that the cake cutting be done right after the bridal party entrance into the reception hall. That way the wait staff can cut the cake and serve it for desert. This prevents having a lot of cake left over at the end of the night.

Second, suggest the couple do their first dance after the cake cutting. This is because the guests are all seated and not milling about as they do after dinner when the first dance is typically done. This way the focus is on the bridal couple.

Then give the bridal couple your time schedule sheet of events:

- **Arriving and entrance—*20 minutes***: Depends upon the bride using the restroom, how long the DJ arranges and talks with the bridal party, who goes to get a drink from the bar and how soon the guests get seated inside.

- **Toast and prayer—*10 to 20 minutes***: Depends upon how many speakers

- **Dinner—*45 minutes to an hour***: Plated or buffet

- **Visiting the guest tables—*5 minutes per table***—Suggest that you will follow the bridal couple to each table to take photos of them with their guests.

- **Cake cutting—*10 minutes***: Take photos of the couple holding the knife to the cake, turning and smiling at you, and cutting the first piece and feeding each other. Ask that they not shove the cake into each other's face until you're done.

- **The Dances—*20 minutes***: First dance, father/daughter, mother/son, bridal party, and other family members.

- **Dancing through the night—*two hours***

- **Garter and bouquet toss—*15 minutes***.

9.6 Event & Portrait Photography

Event photography differs from weddings, bar-bat mitzvahs, and quinceaneras in the respect—that most events are a shorter time period and not as stressful.

The following are the example of events and suggested pricing. However, you should research what other companies are charging and price yourself accordingly.

COMPANY CHRISTMAS PARTIES

For the first 50 couples or single person—I charged a flat fee of $425.00, which included giving each couple or single person 2—5" x 7"s in a white envelope. After the first 50 couples, I charged $1.00 more per couple or single person.

I used my studio lights, blue 8 ft x 8 ft canvas backdrop and had a one hour time limit. I used Sams Club photo processing which cost me 80¢ for two 5" x 7"s. I did not use imprinted photo holders with the company name and event date. Companies did not want to pay the extra $1.00 per folder.

AWARD & DINNER CEREMONIES

I charged a flat fee of $325.00 for two hours as the company only wanted the edited DVD. I used my external flash set up and took photos of people receiving awards on stage, the speakers, hand shaking, table shots of people and any product exhibited.

ON LOCATION PHOTOGRAPHY

When I lived in Arizona, people from the Midwestern and eastern states would visit relatives at holidays. I would be hired at Thanksgiving, Christmas, and Easter to take photos at homes where the families were visiting. I charged $175.00, had a one hour time limit, and gave the family up to 36—4" x 6" hard copies. I did not give the edited CD as I would upload the photos to on-line viewing for ordering enlargements. I used my flash set up and the Gary Fong diffuser and could cover three jobs in one day.

I had the same pricing for high school seniors, pets, babies, etc. on location and in my home studio.

Chapter 10 B & W Developing & Printing

<u>10.1 B & W Film</u>

Back in the day when film was king, developing B & W film and printing on photo paper was the standard college coursework. Today, digital photography and computer printing has relegated B & W to the fine art photography category.

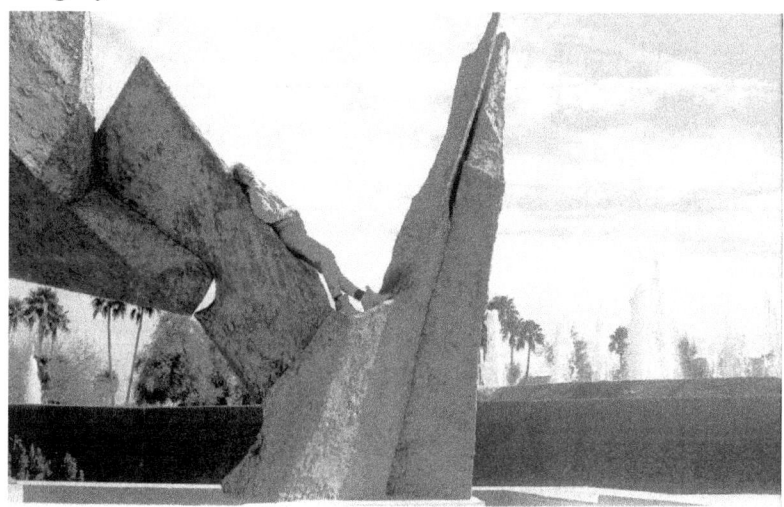

L. L. Smith 1992 Girl on Rock

In school I shot with Kodak Tri-X 400 ISO film. ISO is an acronym for International Standards Organization and means the same as ASA, American Standards Association. With B & W film the higher the ISO number the more sensitive the emulsion is to light and as the ISO rating increases. So does the sensitivity, graininess, and silver content of the negatives.

Below are four of the more common brands of B & W film.

- Kodak ISO 125 Pan X film

- Kodak ISO 400 Tri X film

- Illford ISO 125 and 400

- Fuji Neopan ISO 100—120 film and ISO 400—35 mm film

I would develop between seven to ten roles of B & W film a week—and made hundreds of prints over a two year period using Illford Fiber Base (FB) 8" x 10" photo paper.

When I first began shooting Tri X at 400 ASA, the gray and black areas were defined, but the white areas lacked definition. When printing, I first exposed the entire paper at F/8 for 10 seconds. I then would do a dodge and burn in over the white areas on the print to bring out more definition.

Dodge and burning in was done by cupping my hands together and leaving a slit in between the sides of my palms and using my elbow to push the light switch on and off on the wall. The slit allowed just enough enlarger light through as I moved my hand over the white areas on the print.

When my photography instructor saw me dodging and burning in my prints—he suggested shooting the Tri X at a 200 ASA on my camera and developing the negatives at 6 minutes 50 seconds. This was 20% less than the film package directions of 9 minutes and 6 seconds for shooting at 400 ASA. The result was that the light, gray, and black areas were balanced out and I no longer had to dodge and burn in the white areas.

However, when shooting the Kodak Tri-X 100—leave the ASA setting on your camera at 100.

10.2 Film, Chemicals & Equipment

The B & W film, developing equipment and photo paper in the section can be purchased at **Adorama.com**.

Label all processing chemical containers. Do not handle the chemicals with your fingers—use the tongs and wear gloves. Wear safety goggles to protect your eyes from splashes. Wear old clothing or an apron as the chemicals stain material. Do not store chemicals in the house refrigerator but in a locked cabinet or refrigerator. Fixer turns yellow over time and maybe mistaken for a favored drink.

Here are the chemicals I used for developing and printing:

Kodak D76 developer—This is used for both developing and printing and is available in either the one quart or the one gallon packages. If you are only developing one or two rolls of film and printing only a few prints a week, the quart size should be sufficient. On the other hand if you plan upon developing and printing often, the gallon size is more economical.

Kodak fixer—Is used for both developing and printing and is available in both quart and gallon packets, or in a ready to use liquid. Fixer can be reused 2 to 3 times before discarding. There are salvage kits to reclaim the silver the fixer removes from off the negatives. Do not spill fixer on clothes or carpet as it will bleach out the color and leave a white mark.

One bottle of Orbit bath—Obit bath is used to remove all the fixer off the film.

One bottle of Photo Flo—This removes any water spots right before you hang your negatives up to dry. Do the Photo Flo rinse by where you will be hanging your negatives.

Film Developing Equipment

Time is everything when developing negatives. A large clock with a minute sweep hand should be where it can be seen. Wearing and using a wrist watch is impractical because of agitating the tank with your hands. The needed items are:

1 developing tank kit.[19] The Adorama photo here shows a Paterson developing tank, adjustable white plastic reel on a black spool

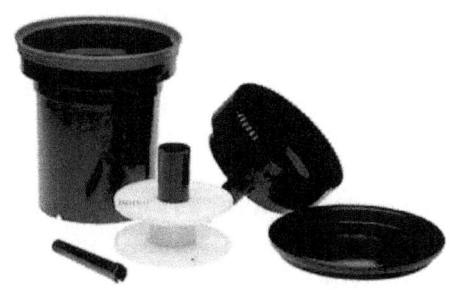

reel holder, light tight proof cover—this is the cylinder shaped item sitting next to the developing tank. It is locked into position over the reels and then the watertight lid is place over the opening.

You can fit two reels of 35 mm film into the canister. A reel can also be expanded to accommodate one roll of medium format film.

Medium format film is used to achieve higher definition photographs. It comes in 120—12 or 16 exposure and 220, 24 or 32 exposure depending upon camera brand. The negative size is either 2.5" x 2.5" square or a 1.34" x 2.5" rectangular shaped for use in a 645 medium format camera.

Three one gallon plastic heavy duty pitchers—Two are used to mix developer and fixer separately. The third one is to pour in the used fixer after the third use.

Four one quart measuring containers—The first one is for the prewash and rinse water after developing. The developing temperature is 68^0. The second container is used for preparing the developer to pour into the tank. The third container is used for mixing the Orbit bath and the fourth container is for mixing the Photo Flo.

Two wooden spoons—One to mix the developer and one to mix the fixer. Do not use metal spoons.

A funnel—To pour the used fixer into one of the gallon containers

One photography thermometer—This has the temperature markings for both B & W and color developing.

A wire clothes hanger and clothes pins—Fold one end of the negative strip over the flat bottom part of the coat hanger and secure with a clothes pin. Then place a clothes pin at the bottom of the negative strip to keep the strip straight. Have this ready before starting to develop film—by hanging the hanger with clothes pins on it from a shower head or shower curtain rack.

Negative film holder sheets—To store the cut negative strips.

Print Making Equipment

The following equipment is needed:

The D-76 and fixer used for developing negatives is also used for printing photographs. When printing—the developer, stop bath, and fixer should be at 68^0.

An enlarger—This can either be a used one or new. There are expensive and economy models. The two popular brands are Beseler and Omega. This Adorama photo is of the Beseler Cadet II B & W 35 mm film enlarger with Lens and negative carrier.[20]

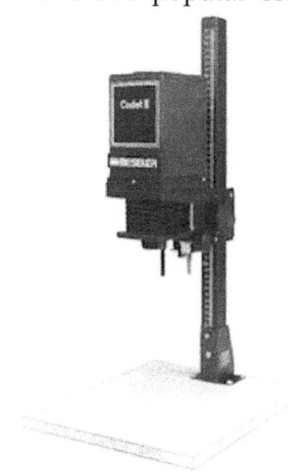

It has a 50 mm lens with adjustable f/stops, a 35 mm negative carrier, an optical glass condenser and enlarging lamp and a filter drawer for 3" x 3" filters.

Multi-contrast filters are used to give more contrast to a print when a negative is too thin from being underexposed. According to Illford: *"A yellow 00 filter has the lowest contrast and a magenta 5 filter has the highest contrast. The 00-3 1/2 filters do not require a change in exposure time. The 4, 4.5, and 5 size filters need twice the exposure time. For example, if you are using a 4.5 filter you will need 20 seconds at f 5.6 when making a print".*[21] (Illford 2014).

You may have to secure your paper easel down with tape to hold it steady after focusing.

When not using the enlarger, cover it with a 30 gallon black trash bag and seal it with masking tape between sessions. If left uncovered dust will get into the light chamber and when printing the dust particles will show up on the print. Then you have to use Marshalls Spotting liquid to dab the white spots.

A stand alone photo developer timer—This is used to time the developer light when it is on. You can also count the seconds as soon as you turn on the developer light by saying 1 one thousand, 1 two thousand, etc.

Five 8" x 10" developing trays—One is for the developer, the second one is for the stop bath after developer, the third one is for the fixer, the fourth one is for the second rinse and the fifth one in the bathtub is for rinsing the prints.

Four photo printing tongs—During print developing keep the tongs in their respective trays to avoid cross contamination with the other chemicals.

One tong is used to pick up the print out of the developing solution to place into the second tray stop bath. The second tong is used to take the print from the stop bath water and place into the fixer tray. The third tong is used to move the print from the fixer to the second rinse tray. The fourth tong is used to move the print to the tray in the bathtub.

A red safety photo light—There are standalones and the type that look like a flood light that screw into a lamp or bathroom light socket.

An 11" x 14" print drying book—The prints are laid in between the pages and it takes about two hours to dry.

A box of either 5" x 7" or 8" x 10" photo paper

- Illford Multigrade IV RC Portfolio Resin Coated VC Variable Contrast Black and White Pearl Surface which takes 1.5 minutes to develop.

- Illford Multigrade IV FB Fiber Based VC Variable Contrast Double weight Black and White Paper which take about three minutes to develop.

10.3 Reeling in the Film

Mix the D-76 developer and fixer according to package directions in the morning. This is because the temperature of the water temperature for mixing the chemicals is about 125^0 and it needs to cool to 68^0 for developing the negatives.

Film processing temperature is 68^0 for the prewash, D-76 developer, and rinse water. The fixer, fixer rinse water, Orbit bath, and Photo Flo can be at room temperature.

For a film camera with a manual rewind crank, rewind the crank slowly while listening to the clicking. When the clicking stops, the end tab is still sticking out of the film canister. This allows for the negative strip end to be cut across and the flat end can be started into the film reel.

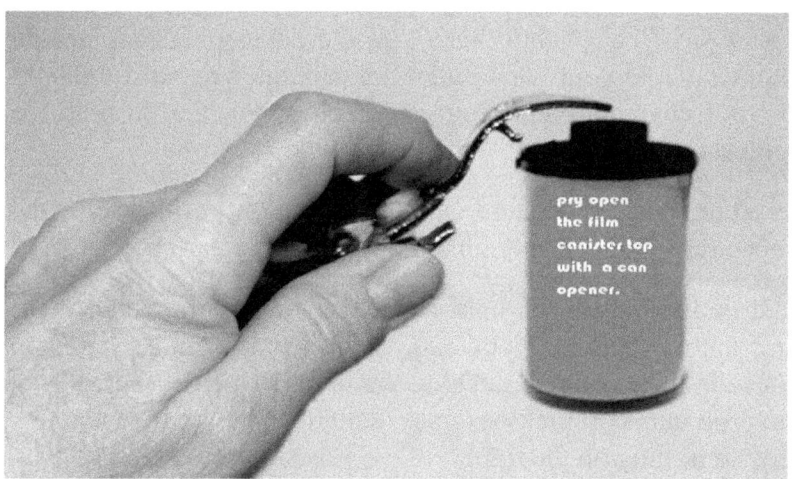

pry open the film canister top with a can opener.

L. L. Smith 2014 Prying off the film canister lid

An automatic rewind camera will not leave the tab hanging out. Take a can opener and pry off the top of the film canister to remove the film. This has to be done in a windowless dark room with no red safe light on. Lay a towel across the bottom of the door to block out any incoming light.

Before loading a reel of B & W in total darkness, buy an inexpensive roll of color film to practice in the light following these steps:

- Practice prying off the film canister top to remove the roll of film. Do not unroll the film and remove from the film spool. Trim the unattached end of the film tab straight across.

- Start the cut end of the film into the white reel going past the first silver balls. Then while gripping the left edge of the reel, twist the right reel edge clockwise to advance the film through the film reel groves.

- When the film is wound all the way through the reel—cut off the film spool and place the reel onto the black reel spool. Place the spool into the tank.

- Place the light tight cover inside the canister and give about a 1/4 t o 1/2 turn clockwise gently until it clicks into place. Even though there is a drainage hole in light proof cover, when the center column is place, it is light tight. To make sure it is locked into place turn the developing tank upside down. Hold your hand under the tank opening so if the light proof cover falls out you can catch it. Put the lid onto the tank.

Practice this procedure until you are confident in the procedure, and can assemble the canister in a dark room.

Before turning off the light in the darkroom, arrange all items in front of you where you can reach them. If you set items on the side then you risk pushing the items onto the floor. If you do drop items on the floor make sure the lid is on the film tank before turning on the light.

10.4 Mixing Chemicals to Develop Film

For developing you need to bring the temperate of both the developer and water to 68 degrees. Since temperatures of the water coming out of the tap vary, the best recommendation is to cool two quarts of water in the refrigerator. You can use any water container instead of your measuring graduates.

Each 35 mm film requires a 1:1 ratio of mixing 4 oz of developer with 4 oz of water or. One roll of medium format film requires 5 oz developer and 5 oz of water. Two rolls of 35 mm film require 8 oz of developer and 8 oz of water:

1. For one 35mm roll, pour 4 oz of developer into a graduate and leave out at room temperature. Place your thermometer in the developer and check the temperature every few minutes until it reaches 68 degrees.

2. While waiting for the developer to reach 68 degrees, prepare the prewash and rinse water. Fill one quart graduate half full with cool tap water. If it is warmer than 68 degrees add more cool refrigerated water until it drops to 68 degrees. Then check the temperature. Alternate this step until you have two quart graduates filled.

3. When the developer is 68 degrees open the lid on the tank and pour in 10 oz of the prewash water. Replace the lid. Pick up the tank and agitate it upside down and right side up continuously for one minute with both hands.

4. Pour out the prewash and find a starting point on the clock and pour in the developer. Agitate the tank continuously for 45 seconds. Then as you watch the clock, quickly and gently tap the bottom of the tank three times on towel.

    Tapping releases air bubbles from the films surface. Do not bang the tank against a hard surface as this can crack the tank.

5. After tapping, set the tank down, instead of holding it for the remainder of the five seconds. The heat from hands can increase the developer temperature.

6. Then pick up the tank and agitate for 30 seconds, tap the tank, and set down for five seconds.

7. Repeat this process for *6 minutes and 50 seconds and no longer*. With developer, every second counts. Going as little as one to two seconds longer than required can change the density of the negative.

8. When the developing time is up pour out the developer and pour in 10 ounces of the prewash water to cover the reel(s) and agitate for 20 seconds. Repeat this process two more times to ensure all developer is removed.

9. Next while watching the clock, pour in enough fixer to cover the reel(s). (Which about half a tank). Fixer removes the silver from the negatives.

10. Agitate the fixer for a minute and then tap the canister three times and set down for the remainder of the 15 seconds.

11. Then agitate the tank 30 seconds, tap, set down for 15 seconds. Repeat this process for three minutes.

12. When finished take off the lid and pour the fixer into the used fixer container using a funnel to avoid spills. Pour in rinse water and agitate for one minute. Repeat this process two times.

13. Now you can remove the light tight cover and place the tank under running water for one minute. Then remove the film spool and take off the white reel. Look at the negatives by pulling out a section of the negatives carefully from the reels. Hold the negatives up to the light. It should look like the negative image on the next page. The blacks, grays and whites all have contrast and definition. Then twist the negatives back onto the reel and place the reel back onto the spool.

14. Next dip the reel into the Orbit bath and agitate up and down for one minute. When done put the spool and reel back into the tank and put back under running water for four minutes. Wash your hands to remove any chemical residue for the next step.

15. After rinsing the film take the tank to the area where the negatives are to be hung on the hanger. (Preferably in the shower). Take the reel off the film spool and twist to

separate the reel. Next take the negative strip and dip it up and down through the Photo Flo for 30 seconds. This will prevent water spots.

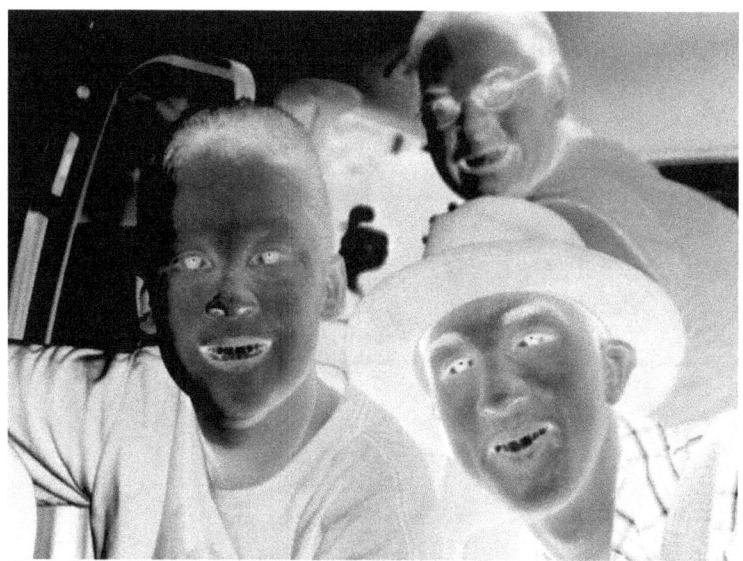

L. L. Smith 2011 Negative Example

16. Before hanging, pull the film strip upwards with your dominant hand between the index and middle finger on your non dominant hand. You should have no developing chemical residue on your fingers. The negatives can also be hung right up after dipping in Photo Flo without running through the fingers.

17. Fold over onto the flat part of the coat hanger, the end of the negative strip with the area that is void of photos. Use a clothes pin to hold it in place. Use another clothes pin to weigh down the bottom edge of the negative strip. This keeps the strip straight. It takes about six hours for the strip to dry.

18. Once dry cut between a negative every fifth frame and use negative holder sheets to store the negatives.

10.5 Printing—Using the Enlarger

You will need to set up both the enlarger and your trays of printing chemicals in the same area.

The work flow diagram below is for a bathroom darkroom set up. If you have the screw in flood style of red safety light— screw it into the light socket above the sink.[22]

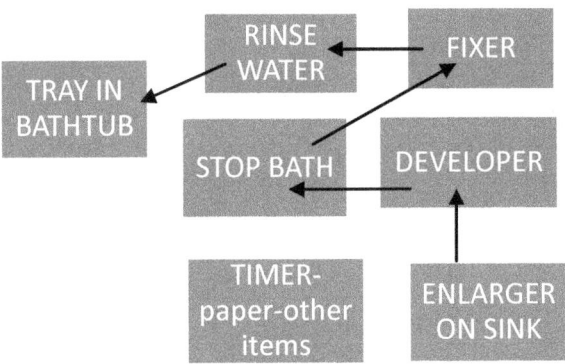

When the enlarger aperture is wide open with the lamp on, it is bright enough to turn photo paper black that is not in the light tight bag. Use the red safety light as your working light source when you are removing photo paper from the light protective bag. Always fold the bag flap over and put the paper back into the box before turning on the enlarger light.

The enlarger lens turns back and forth and has f/stop numbers of f/2.8, f/4, f/5.6, f/8, f/11, f/16 that you should know in that order. The f/stop of f/2.8 is wide open and allows the most light to come through. This is setting to use when focusing the negative on the photo paper holder. The smallest aperture is f/16 which is the closed down setting.

When exposing the paper the ideal setting is f/8 which reduces the time the enlarger light stays on. The first time I printed I used f/11 at 20 seconds. When my instructor noticed he commented, "You know that's too long, any movement like an earth tremor will make your print blurry. Try f/8 at 10 seconds." I did and it worked for me.

As shown on the negative image on the top of the next page, the negative is placed into the holder emulsion side down with the ID numbers up.

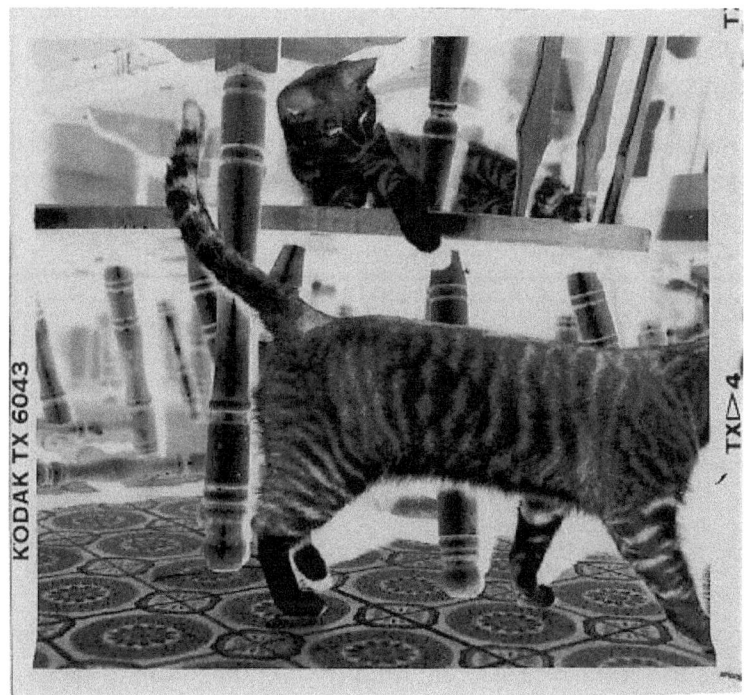

L. L. Smith 1989 In focus negative example

Focusing is done by setting the negative into the negative holder and then pulling down a lever to open the area between the lens housing and bellows. Set the negative holder inside, close the opening, and focus the negative by opening the lens aperture to f/2.8 to project the brightest amount of light.

Place your paper easel onto the baseboard and adjust the enlarger up until the negative fits the inside paper easel boarders. Turn the focusing knob slowly until you see the grains of the negative, which look like up close sand grains.

The image above is what an in focus negative should look like. The ID numbers and boarder should not be visible.

Next turn the lens back down to F/8 and turn off the enlarger light before making a test strip or contact full sheet print.

Contact sheets are the way to see which prints you would like to make. A contact sheet is made by laying your negative sheet holder over a sheet of RC 8" x 10" photo paper. Expose the paper for 3 seconds at F/5.6 and then develop the paper for 1.5 minutes, rinse 1 minute, fix for 3 minutes, and rinse 5 minutes. This is enough to see the images on the paper.

Before making your first full size print of any negative, make a test strip. Take a sheet of photo paper and cut it into three-4" strips the length of the paper using the light from the red safety light. Place all the strips back into the light protective bag, fold over the flap, and place the bag back into the box.

Next do the negative focusing process. Don't forget to turn the f/2.8 aperture setting back to f/8, and turn off the enlarger lamp. Take out one of the 4" test strips from the light protective bag and place into the middle of the easel. Then turn on the enlarger light for 10 seconds to expose the strip then develop.

After you rinse it, just enough to get the chemicals off, look at it to determine if you need less or more seconds. If the test strip is too light increase the time two seconds longer then do another test strip. The print on page 160 shows an evenly balanced B & W print.

Making a Print

The printing process uses chemicals that absorb into the skin and stains clothes, carpet, tile, and furniture. So be safe by following a few simple steps.

Use an old desk such as one of those flat top grade school desks to avoid staining good furniture. This style of desk fits the four 8" x 10" trays. The trays, tongs, and paper can be stored in the slot under the top between developing sessions. The chemicals do absorb into your skin. Use the tongs to move prints from one tray to another instead of your fingers. When finished with a developing session, wash your hands.

During printing when lifting photo paper out of a tray, don't shake the paper but let the fluids run/drip off the paper back into the tray.

Preparing the trays

1. The chemicals and rinse waters should be at 68 degrees. Use a clock with a second sweep hand so you can accurately time each step of the printing process.

2. Fill one tray with developer, one with fixer and three with rinse water. The first tray can be either stop bath chemical or water which stops the developing process on the paper.

3. On the table place the developer, stop bath, fixer, and rinse water trays as show in the diagram on page 156 for a smooth work flow.

4. Have a light steady stream of water running into the tray in the tub. This will keep the water refreshed to rinse away the chemicals. Let the prints rinse for at least 20 minutes before placing them into the print drying book.

5. Use the photo paper developing times recommended on the box. Most RC Resin Coated printing papers takes 1.5 minutes to develop. FB Fiber Based Paper takes about three minutes to develop. Make sure to agitate the tray back and forth gently and constantly to keep the paper covered. Be careful not to spill out the chemicals.

6. After the time is up use the tongs and move the paper to the stop bath tray and agitate the print for 30 seconds.

7. Next move the print to the fixer tray for three minutes and agitate constantly.

8. Then move the print to the rinse water tray for one minute and agitate. Then move the print to the tray in the tub.

9. When finished developing prints, rinse the prints for about 20 minutes under running water, making sure the prints are not sticking together.

10. Remove the print from the water and gently shake the water off the print, and then place them into the print drying book. It should take about two hours for prints to dry for the plastic paper, six hours if fiber based.

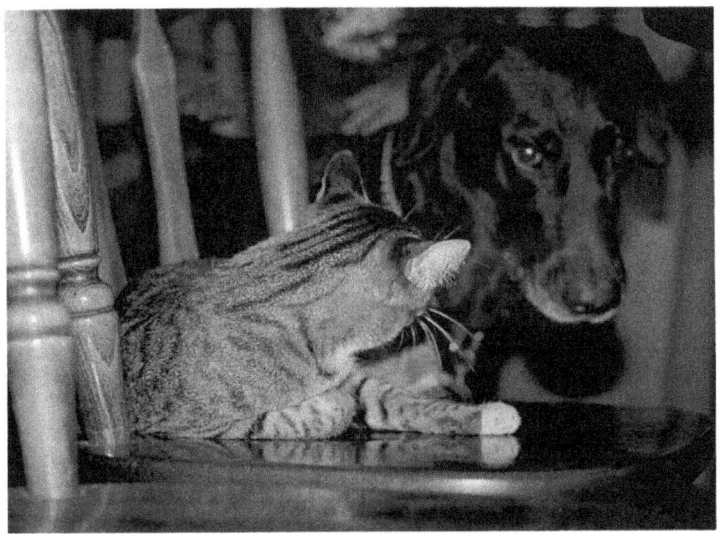

L. L. Smith 1989 Cat & dog stare down

Touching up your prints

Marshalls Neutral Black Spot liquid will remove white dust spots on prints. You will need a No. 000 or finer sable brush, small cup of water, small ceramic plate, and a fine soft cloth.

Dip the brush bristles into the Marshalls liquid, remove, and dab the liquid onto the plate. Put the lid back on the solution to prevent spills and stains. Dip the brush into the water and then mix with the spotting fluid to thin it out.

Next, look for the darkest area on the photo where the spot is. Then dab the tip of the brush into the thinned mixture and dab the print. If the dabbed spot is darker then the area—use the soft cloth to dab it off before it dries.

Thin out the spotting fluid with more dabs of water as you progress to the lighter areas.

When spotting a line, dab the length of the line instead of brushing. If you don't like how the print looks—you can re-rinse the print for ten minutes and then let it dry.

Mounting Prints

When entering prints in juried competitions or framed for shows, the prints need to be printed on fiber based paper and mounted onto acid free rag board. Rag board can be purchased from stores that sell art supplies. Also needed is a package of mounting tissue, two thin hand towels, and a six inch ruler.

This is the size of rag board recommended for prints.

Print size	Rag board size
5" x 7"	8" x 10"
8" x 10"	11" x 14"
11" x 14"	16" x 20"
16" x 20"	20" x 24"

Dry mount presses with a temperature setting of 120^0- 125^0 is used to mount the photos onto the rag board. However, the cost of a heat mounting press will set you back over $1000.00. But you can improvise using a clothes iron and an expendable FB print. Do not use good prints when practicing this method.

Use the irons lowest heat setting with the steam setting turned off. A high heat setting will cause the print to crease and curdle and look wavy, ruining the print.

Lay one of hand towels on the ironing board and lay the photo paper on the towel. Next place a piece of print mounting tissue onto the back of the practice print. Then using the tip of the iron, touch the tissue at opposite corners of the photo and press it down gently for three seconds. Check the tissue to see if it is attached to the print back. If not apply the iron again.

Next the rag board on the towel on the iron board and center the print with tissue paper down on the rag board. Measure from the edge of the print to the edge of the rag board with the ruler to check that the distance is even on all sides. Then lift the one unattached corners while holding the print down in the middle and use the iron to press the tissue down onto the mount board. Do the same for the other corner.

Next lay the other towel over the print. Lay the iron flat on one corner of the print and start moving the iron across the towel in a firm but gentle motion, back and forth moving down the entire length of the print.

When done look the print to check if it is attached. Gently curve the rag with both hands. If the print is not attach it will rise off the rag board. If not attached—repeat the above maneuver.

The frames sold in a big box store are not suitable for framing a print to be exhibited or selling to a client. The print should be custom framed in a mat. That way the print will not come in contact with the glass and get stuck. You see this with color prints in inexpensive store bought frames with glass.

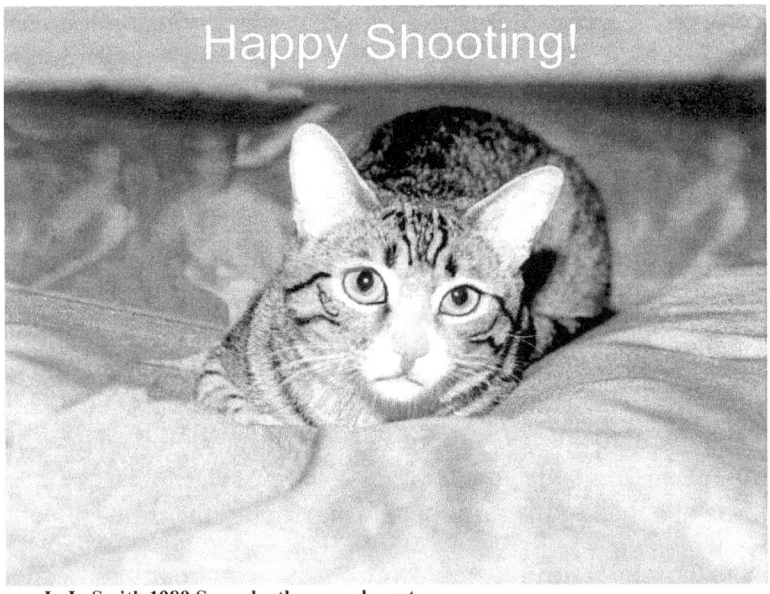

L. L. Smith 1989 Squeaky the grouchy cat

Appendix
Photography website resources
Albums, Photo
- www.Renaissancealbums.com
- www.topflightalbums.com
- www.weddingalbumsandmore.com
- www.weddingalbumdepot.com

Album making software
- www.garyfongstore.com

Backdrops
- www.backdropoutlet.com
- www.dennymfg.com

Books & Gifts
- www.blurb.com/partner/jalbum
- www.createspace.com/
- www.portraitweavers.com
- www.MyPublisher.com

Black & white film printing
- www.ilfordphoto.com/products/default.asp

Business Cards, Postcards, Calendars, Pens
- www.vistaprint.com
- www.pens.com

Business Leads/reciprocal websites
- www.allseasonsweddings.com/wedding-link-exchange
- www.blooming.briderush.com
- www.brideappeal.com/home
- www.mywedding.com/apps/public/content/advertising
- www.Respond.com
- www.theknot.com
- www.twitter.com/FreeWeddingLead
- www.wedalert.com/
- www.weddingblogs100.com/advertise-with-us.html
- www.weddingchannel.com
- www.wedj.com/dj-photo-video.nsf/banners.html
- www.yourbridalplanner.com

Business Networking Groups
- www.toastmasters.org/
- www.bni.com/
- www.uschamber.com/

Business Resources
- www.sba.gov/tools/sba-learning-center/search/training/ starting-business
- www.business.ftc.gov/documents/bus69-protecting-personal -information-guide-business
- www.irs.gov/Businesses/Small-Businesses-&-Self-Employed/Starting-a-Business
- www.legalzoom.com
- www.quickbooks.intuit.com

Contest Sites
- www.pfmagazine.com
- www.travel.nationalgeographic.com/travel/traveler-magazine/photo-contest/2014
- www.nikon-photocontest.com/en/#/home

Editing software
- www.adobe.com
- www.tv.adobe.com/show/learn-lightroom-4
- www.autofx.com/products/mttc/detail.html
- www.corel.com/corel/allProducts.jsp
- www.en.softonic.com/s/virtual-painter-5
- www.photoshop.com
- www.pinnaclesys.com/publicsite/us/home

Editing websites—Free to use
- www.fotoflexer.com
- www.fotor.com
- www.picmonkey.com
- www.134.lunapic.com/editor
- www.pixlr.com
- www.ribbet.com
- www.tucia.com

Email newsletters—Free or low cost
- www.search.constantcontact.com
- www.mailchimp.com

Flash & Studio Lighting
- www.garyfongstore.com
- www.lumedyne.com/products/BATTERIES.ASP
- www.speedotron.com/products

Google Search Engine Optimization (SEO) tools
- www.google.com/webmasters/
- www.support.google.com/webmasters/answer/70897

On line proofing sites
- www.bludomain.com/
- www.collages.net/
- www.photoproofpro.com/
- www.digiproofs.com/
- www.shootproof.com/
- www.imagequix.com/iq
- www.pictage.com
- www.picturespro.com
- www.zenfolio.com

Organizations, Photographic
- www.findapro.kodak.com
- www.ppa.com
- www.worldpressphoto.org/

Photo Equipment
- www.adorama.com
- www.bhphotovideo.com
- www.samsclub.com/

Social Media& Photographic communities
- www.ephotozine.com/
- www.facebook.com
- www.linkedin.com/
- www.photographysites.com/
- twitter.com/FreeWeddingLead
- http://photo.net/
- www.picturesocial.com/
- www.photography.com/

Stock sites
- www.alamy.com
- www.art.com/
- www.artistrising.com/
- www.istockphoto.com/
- www.photostockplus.com/
- www.submitstockphotos.com
- www.contributor.corbis.com/knowledgebase
- www.contributors.gettyimages.com/
- www.bigstockphoto.com/
- www.us.fotolia.com
- www.veer.com

<u>Tutorials</u>
- www.digital-photography-school.com/rule-of-thirds
- www.istockphoto.com/help/sell-stock/training-manuals/photography/istocks-standards
- www.luminous-landscape.com/tutorials/zone_system.shtml
- www.photographytips.com/page.cfm/4875
- www.nikonusa.com/Learn-And-Explore/Photography-Techniques/g3cu6o1r/1/Understanding-Maximum-Aperture.html
- www.photo.stackexchange.com/questions/6495/in-portrait-photography-what-is-broad-lighting-what-is-short-lighting)
- www.tv.adobe.com/show/learn-lightroom-4/

<u>Web site building programs & hosting</u>
- www.bludomain.com/ *Starts at $50.00*
- www.clickbooq.com/ *Offers a 14 day free trial*
- www.godaddy.com/
- http://intothedarkroom.com/ *Photography websites, blogs, photo carts, slideshows, hosting and more*
- www.jalbum.net
- www.jimdo.com
- www.photobiz.com
- www.portfoliositez.com
- www.wix.com/stunningwebsites
- www.squarespace.com
- www.smugmug.com
- www.weebly.com
- www.wordpress.com

<u>Laura L. Smith websites</u>
- www.fineartamerica.com/art/all/laura+smith/all
- www.clickingforcashfromhome.com/
- www.youtube.com/watch?v=FDKis0aoBHY

References

1. Anonymous. Nikon USA. Learn and Explore. Understanding Maximum Aperture. Para. 1. 2014. Retrieved April 14, 2014 from http://www.nikonusa.com/Learn-And-Explore/ Photography-Techniques/g3cu6o1r/1/Understanding-Maximum-Aperture.html

2. Speedotron lights. Photo. 2014. B & H Photo. Retrieved April 14, 2014 from http://www.bhphotovideo.com/c/product/ 50021- REG/Speedotron_11275_1205CX_2_CC_Head. html

3. Light dome. Photoflex Corp. Photo. 2014. Photoflex Products. Retrieved April 14, 2014 from https://www.photoflex.com/ products/litedome-large

4. Smith Victor mini slave. Photo. 2014. Adorama. Retrieved April 14, 2014 from http://www.adorama.com/SVPG6S.html

5. Table top studio in a bag. Photo. 2014. Adorama. Retrieved April 14, 2014 from http://www.adorama.comVRDSB1616. html

6. Interfit Photographic FM-01, Digital Incident and Reflected Flash Meter. Photo. 2014. Adorama. Retrieved April 14, 2014 from http://www.adorama.com/PAIFM01.html

7. Puckett, E. A. Family on Couch 1. Photo. 2011.

8. Puckett, E. A. Family on Couch 2. Photo. 2011.

9. Anonymous. Stack Exchange. In Portrait photography, what is 'broad' lighting? What is 'short' lighting? Photo Stack Exchange. January 06, 2011. Retrieved April 14, 2014 from http://photo.stackexchange.com/questions/6495/in-portrait-photography-what-is-broad-lighting -what-is-short-lighting)

10. Anonymous. Getty Images. What are our technical requirements 1998-2014. Contributor Resource. Getty Image Contributor Community. Retrieved April 14, 2014 from http://contributors.gettyimages.com/article_public.aspx? article_id=2371Getty Images ?

11. Anonymous. Corbis. Work with Us. 1998-2014. Contributor Gateway. 2014. http://contributor.corbis.com/workwithus

12. Anonymous. Corbis. Image Check Script 1998-2014. Corbis Image Contributor Community Knowledge Base. Retrieved April 14, 2014 from http://contributor.corbis.com/ knowledgebase#Tutorials

13. Ziglar, Zig. Official Ziglar Quotes. The Official Quote Library. Para. 15. 2014. Retrieved April 14, 2014 from http://www.ziglar.com/

14. Tyndell Photographic. Thrifty Choice Album. Photo. 2014. Retrieved April 14, 2014 from https://www.tyndellphoto graphic.com/product/albums/thrifty-choice-album/395-2

15. Vista Print Business Card example. 2013

16. Banner Image. WeDj. Link to us for better SEO. Para. 8. Taken from http://www.wedj.com/dj-photo-video.nsf/banners.html.

17. Anonymous. Google. Do You Need an SEO, para. 19. 2014. Google Webmaster Tools. Retrieved April 14, 2014 from https://support.google.com/webmasters/answer/35291?hl=en

18. Anonymous. Google. Do You Need an SEO, para. 6. 2014. Google Webmaster Tools. Retrieved April 14, 2014 from https://support.google.com/webmasters/answer/35291?hl=en

19. Patterson developing tank. Photo. 2014. Adorama. Retrieved April 14, 2014 from http://www.adorama.com

20. Beseler Cadet II B & W 35 mm film enlarger. Photo. 2014. Adorama. Retrieved April 14, 2014 from http://www.adorama.com/BEC2.html

21. Anonymous. Illford Photo. Applications printing in Black and White Darkroom Equipment. Current Multigrade Filters. Para. 5 2014. Retrieved April 14, 2014 from http://www.ilfordphoto.com/aboutus/page.asp?n=117

22. Smith, L. L. Darkroom flow chart. Illustration. 2014.

Photographs by Laura L. Smith

No.	Title	Year	Page
1	Lake Powel 37	1996	1
2	Camera Flash Set-up 1	2013	23
3	Camera Flash Set-up 2	2013	24
4	Son, sister, and daughter	2006	25
5	Son and his friend	2007	26
6	Lumedyne battery	2013	27
7	Studio Light set-up pencil sketch	2014	34
8	Daughter holding kitten	1999	34
9	Self portrait of L. L. Smith	2006	35
10	L. L. Smith holding cat	1991	36
11	Pampering the Bride	2008	38
12	Baby lying on blanket	1982	42
13	Man with guitar	2008	43
14	Man by tree	2008	46
15	Dog in dress	1999	47
16	Couple by Mormon Temple, AZ	1999	50
17	Liz in the Sun	1990	52
18	Fill Card drawing	2014	53
19	Author's niece and grandson	1999	54
20	Woman by window 1	2009	54
21	Woman by window 2	2009	54
22	Plated food	2009	59
23	Family Restored	1980	63
24	Cakes on a Plate	2009	65
25	Glass Vase	2006	65
26	Iris and swan	2006	66
27	Fireworks over Niagara Falls	2005	67
28	Antelope Slot Canyon, AZ	2004	68
29	People on the road in Guatemala	2006	70
30	Northern Arizona	2004	71
31	Wupatki Indian Ruins, AZ	2004	72
32	Daisies	2010	73
33	Diamond Back rattlesnake	1998	74
34	Ape in tree, Guatemala	2006	75
35	Superstition Mountains AZ	2011	76
36	People on bridge, Guatemala	2006	77
37	Couple by Lake	2009	104

38	Photo collage layout	2009	105
39	Photo sheet created with FongSoft	2009	123
40	Girl on rock	1992	145
41	Opening a film canister	2014	151
42	Negative example after developing	2013	155
43	In focus negative example	1989	157
44	Cat and dog stare off	1989	160
45	Squeaky the grouchy cat	1989	162

www.ingramcontent.com/pod-product-compliance
Lightning Source LLC
Chambersburg PA
CBHW060850170526
45158CB00001B/301